PROJECTS FROM PINE

33 Plans for the Beginning Woodworker

Dedication

Ann F. Jacobson and Helen M. Park,
My designers and tracers,
With thanks and love

No. 2871
$17.95

PROJECTS FROM PINE

33 Plans for the Beginning Woodworker

James A. Jacobson

TAB BOOKS Inc.
Blue Ridge Summit, PA 17214

FIRST EDITION
FIRST PRINTING

Library of Congress Cataloging in Publication Data

Jacobson, James A.
Projects from pine.

Includes index.
1. Woodwork. I. Title.
TT180.J28 1987   684'.08   87-13886
ISBN 0-8306-7871-9
ISBN 0-8306-2871-1 (pbk.)

Questions regarding the content of this book
should be addressed to:

Reader Inquiry Branch
Editorial Department
TAB BOOKS Inc.
P.O. Box 40
Blue Ridge Summit, PA 17214

Contents

Reasons for Finishing—Preliminaries to Finishing—Types of Finishes—Finishing Procedures—Hanging Devices and Procedures

Acknowledgments

I wish to thank the following companies for providing photographs and granting permission to use them:

Adjustable Clamp Co., Chicago, IL
Borden, Inc., Columbus, OH
Campbell-Hausfeld Co., Harrison, OH
Delta International Machinery Corp., Pittsburgh, PA
Dremel, Division of Emerson Electric Co., Racine, WI
Enco Manufacturing Co., Chicago, IL
Leichtung, Inc., Cleveland, OH
Northwestern Steel and Wire Co., Sterling, IL
Porter-Cable Corp., Jackson, TN
Red Devil, Inc., Union, NJ
Senco Products, Inc., Cincinnati, OH
Stanley Tools, Division of the Stanley Works, New Britain, CT
Warren Tool Co., Rhineback, NY
Woodworks, Ft. Worth, TX
Vermont American Tool Co., Division of Vermont American, Lincolnton, NC

Special acknowledgment and thanks are extended to Peter J. Jacobson for doing all the photographic work for the manuscript and the initial cover design.

Introduction

In recent years, there has been an increasing interest in do-it-yourself projects. For a variety of reasons, including economics, most of us prefer doing as many things around the house as possible. These projects are not only worth doing in themselves, but they also provide a vehicle for the constructive use of our leisure time. Although many of these do-it-yourself projects are a combination of satisfaction and frustration, few result in lifelong hobbies. The intention of do-it-yourself projects is to get something done rather quickly with a minimum of investment and, hopefully, some success and a large degree of satisfaction.

Over the years, I have observed an interest and fascination on the part of many persons to do some woodworking. This interest seems to focus not on complex pieces of furniture, but rather on more mundane items such as shelves, towel hangers, mirrors, and decorative pieces to hang on the walls. There seems a need for a do-it-yourself book that will give individuals the satisfaction of woodworking, but at an achievable skill level and with a minimal investment. Unlike some of us who want to spend all of our time working with wood, many individuals seem more interested in making a few projects that are relatively simple, but yet functional and decorative. This book seeks to meet this need by providing a series of projects that can be made from pine.

In addition to presenting projects that can be readily made by the nonwoodworker, suggestions are also given for those who want to make these designs in quantity to sell at craft shows. Although production work requires some of the larger floor tools, the projects all lend themselves to being made in quantity with relative ease.

The projects presented also permit the homeowner, student, or production woodworker to make pieces that are generally considered "country." In recent years, there has been a national love affair with those things that represent a life-style different from our own. This is exemplified by the extensive and intensive interest in things that are both Early American and rural in theme. The projects presented here are basically country in design. Making your own country projects will give the various pieces an authenticity not found in purchased items. Making your own decorative and functional accessories places you in the mainstream of true American crafting.

Although the projects do not require any decorative embellishments, they can be enhanced by a diversity of methods. Most of the projects are designed to present sufficient surface for tole painting. If you are actively engaged in tole painting, you will find that, with a minimum of effort, you also can make your own projects for painting. Since tole painting is not an area of expertise for me, I have included a Bibliography to assist you in developing skills in this area. Woodburning and carving are two other methods that can be used to enhance the various projects. Pine is ideal for either carving or whittling, along with woodburning to make pieces more attractive. A number of projects will assist you in obtaining some experience with these devices.

Another important emphasis in this book is to encourage you to design your own projects. Suggestions and methods are provided to assist you in this process. The various projects are designed to help you develop confidence in your own abilities. Although you might approach the various tasks as do-it-yourself projects, you might very well end up as a captive to the design and woodworking process.

The kitchen is a good place to begin an inventory process that can be applied to every room in the house. Houses have been designed with an array of rooms, each serving a very different but related function. To demonstrate the inventory process that can be used for planning, the kitchen will serve as our example room. As you begin to explore the range of existing and possible functions of a room, project needs will begin to emerge.

In general, the kitchen lends itself to an endless array of decorative and functional pine accessories. By accessories, I mean those items that add attractiveness or convenience to a room, but that are not essential to its purpose. In other words, when constructed, kitchens are fully equipped with cabinets, a range, refrigerator, sink, counters, and possibly, a dishwasher and microwave. These items are essential to the primary purpose of the kitchen. However, how barren and cold a kitchen would be with only those things that fulfill its basic function. It is clearly the accessories—those interesting and different things that are placed or hung on walls—that make the kitchen a warm and pleasant environment. The very nature of a kitchen is enhanced by a wide variety of items, especially wood pieces selectively placed. Wood, as kitchen cabinets so visually display, is very much at home in the kitchen.

The curious thing about wood accessories in the kitchen is that nothing needs to match. It is indeed the one room in the house that easily can display a conglomerate of things that create warmth, comfort, and function. Stains, paints, finishes, and types of wood do not need to match. Tole-painted pieces blend with water colors and children's school pictures. Oak cabinets are never embarrassed for a pine shelf. The kitchen is truly the catch-all room that reflects the myriad interests, tastes, smells, whims, humor, and values of all those who spend time there. In a very real sense, the kitchen is an extension and portrait of a family's personality.

In thinking about the kitchen, it is of interest to note that it is the one room in almost every house where guests and family feel the most comfortable. Inevitably guests, friends, and even strangers are ushered into the kitchen. Most homes have well-appointed living rooms, but it is the kitchen that is most often used. There is an atmosphere of informality and relaxation that is unique to kitchens. Conversation is easier and more comfortable. Social barriers tend to fall more quickly. People are always willing to have coffee or a drink in the kitchen. Unlike the tidy living room, perpetual clutter in the kitchen enhances and warms the interpersonal encounters. Much of this environment, next to the individuals themselves, seems to be created by all those interesting items that adorn our kitchens.

In addition to being the primary room for socialization, the kitchen is also the primary working center of the house. Convenience and maximum use of minimum space is the rule. Things, of necessity, must be somewhat ordered, and places to put items are mandatory. As with closets, kitchens never seem large enough for all that is demanded of them. Contractors seem to have little sense of space and design needs for a kitchen, not to mention its many functions. Although many persons would like to redesign and remodel their kitchen, few can afford it. Not only is the remodeling often too expensive but a kitchen, by its very nature and function, cannot be closed down to accommodate its reconstruction.

Accessories made from pine often can supplant the need to remodel or redesign the kitchen. Appropriate pieces that have function, yet are decorative, can forestall the immediate desire or need to remodel. Although core items that are permanent fixtures cannot be altered significantly, they can be greatly enhanced with various self-made projects. Where cabinet space is limited, shelves or open cabinets can be built and hung. Treasures and everyday pieces that were kept in the cupboard can be displayed and made accessible on a plate shelf. Cookbooks can be removed from countertops and placed on a shelf made from pine. Peg boards for cups can be built. Sewing supplies can be made readily available by crafting a hanging sewing board. Coats can be hung behind doors on Shaker peg boards. Flowerpots can be hung rather than cluttering windowsills. Towel holders can be made and placed in strategic locations. Hanging boxes neatly tole-painted or woodburned can be appropriately placed or hung.

The changes that can be made in a kitchen through the use of homemade projects are limited only by space and your own imagination. If you are inclined to that country look, projects made from pine are the best way to achieve this effect. As you inventory the various functions and needs in the kitchen, I think you will find a project in this book that you can make or redesign to meet those needs. As you explore functions and needs for other rooms in your house, you will find that a similar inventory of projects will emerge.

The typical bathroom can serve as another example of this inventory process. Although the kitchen has been the target of most home craftsmen, the bathroom is increasingly becoming the room to be enhanced with wood pieces. With the exception of older homes, most homeowners are the victims of bathrooms designed by contractors and furnished by plumbing suppliers. Infrequently are new homes or remodeled ones constructed or designed to include wood accessories in bathrooms. In general, bathroom decor has been dictated by the purveyors of chrome and porcelain. More recently, plastics and other chemical-based products have found their way into bathroom furnishings. Few homeowners, until recently, have been willing to undertake the task of replacing these rather sterile-appearing items with wood pieces of their own making. Also, an increasing number of individuals are insisting that bathrooms in their new homes be appointed with wood accessories they have purchased or plan to make themselves. Wooden accessories, especially those crafted by the homeowner, can radically transform the environment of most bathrooms.

Regrettably, although there are many ideas and examples of wood pieces for the bath available, little attention has been given to the do-it-yourself woodworker. There are no historic designs or models to examine or refer to for assistance. With a bit of imagination, some pine, and a few tools, however, you can transfer a country-type theme to bathroom accessories. While maintaining this theme, you can design bathroom accessories around function.

For example, chrome towel holders can be replaced with ones made from pine. Bath towels can be held on double towel bars with an attached storage shelf for extra towels. An attractive and functional toilet-tissue holder with a small shelf can replace its chrome counterpart. Shaker peg boards can be made and attached to the wall for hanging clothing or robes. Single or multiple peg boards can be secured to doors. A large Shaker shelf with pegs can provide much needed shelf space. A small pine device can be made to hold a hand towel and hair dryer.

As you apply an inventory process to the bath, you will discover a range of pieces, both decorative and functional, that can be made from pine. In exploring current functions and desired functions, a continuing range of new ideas and projects begin to emerge. I think that you will find any number of the projects presented in this book will meet many of these emerging needs.

As you apply a similar inventory process to the family room, a child's bedroom, the dining or living room, a finished basement or hallway, and any other room in your house, a similar range of projects will emerge. If you approach each area both in terms of function and decoration, you will be amazed at the delightful array of projects with which you are confronted. Best of all, you can make most of these projects with a minimal investment of time and resources. Other projects might require a greater time commitment, but yet remain achievable.

It is the intention of this book to help you build, finish, and hang, if needed, the various projects you decide are needed in your house. As suggested, the projects can be made as presented, or they can be redesigned to meet a specific need. In many of the projects, possible optional design considerations are presented.

To make your crafting easier and more informed, information on pine and the selection of lumber for projects is presented in detail. Information and suggestions on tools and their various accessories also are given to assist you in both planning and doing the projects. Sources for specialty items such as Shaker pegs, candle holders, and a range of other items, including tools, are listed as an Appendix. Following the project chapter, a final section details the finishing process from beginning to end. It also includes such necessary information as ways to hang a shelf. To assist you in becoming a more informed woodworker and to provide specialized information, an extensive Bibliography is provided.

Chapter 1

Wood for Projects

Although woodworking can be immensely practical and satisfying, it is the wood itself that makes it all possible. Wood, as you might know, can be an endless source of fascination and pleasure. It is one of those wonderous phenomena of nature that never ceases to interest and fascinate most people. You will discover, as you become involved in woodworking, that much of the pleasure is in learning about the different woods that are available.

Added to this learning process is the very challenging experience of selecting your boards for a particular project. All wood, even the seemingly worthless piece, presents you with an interesting decision-making process as you examine it in relation to a possible project. In many instances, you will discover that the wood you are examining will suggest an object or a project. Before you can explore the process of selecting wood for a particular project, you will need to have some information about wood in general.

Basically, there are two primary groups of wood: the hardwoods and the softwoods. Interestingly enough, these designations have nothing to do with the actual hardness or softness of the wood itself. In fact, some hardwoods are quite soft, while a number of softwoods are rather hard. For example, most wood-carvers prefer working with basswood because it is a very soft wood with a uniform grain. It is easy to carve and is soft enough that a fingernail will readily penetrate its surface. Basswood, however, is designated as a hardwood. The designations of hardwood and softwood have, over a period of years, been generally accepted as representing the two primary categories of wood.

The actual distinctions between woods are, in fact, based on a number of rather technical factors. For example, the type of cell structure in the wood itself is one way of distinguishing between hardwoods and softwoods. The details of cell structure in wood is a very technical area. The Bibliography lists a number of reference books on the subject. You will find other references that will assist you in exploring the fascinating area of the technology of wood. For our purposes, it is sufficient to know that hardwoods and softwoods can be identified rather accurately and easily by their leaves. For example, trees with broad leaves, such as oak, birch, maple, cherry, walnut, hickory, and elm, are generally considered hardwoods. They generally shed their leaves in the fall, and so are called *deciduous*. Trees with needles, such as pine, spruce fir, and other evergreens, are called *conifers,* and are generally classified as softwoods. Another characteristic that distinguishes woods is the amount of sap, or *resin*, they contain. Softwoods generally contain substantial amounts of resin. You also will discover a very real difference between the woods in the marketplace: hardwoods are expensive, softwoods are not.

Although the softwoods, pine in particular, will be the primary wood recommended for most projects, you should begin to become more informed on all the woods. Many books on wood are available for purchase or loan from your local library. Additionally, numerous government publications deal with the technology of wood. A number of references are provided in the Bibliography.

Another source of learning is the craft fairs that almost every community seems to have during the summer. Most people in wood crafts are delighted to share information about woods, their use, sources of supply, and other helpful information. You also might find yourself gleaning a few ideas for projects. I urge you to patronize these local craftsmen.

A final, and probably more exciting, source of learning about woods is your local lumber or hardwood dealer. Most local lumberyards stock primarily softwoods because their customers are usually contractors, homebuilders, and homeowners. They can be very helpful when you go to purchase your material or ask questions. Be careful, however, not to assume that just because they sell lumber that they also know about it. If you have done your homework, in many instances you will be better informed than the employees.

You also might want to locate a hardwood dealer in your area or, if available, a hardwood sawmill. In most instances, hardwood dealers are delighted to spend time answering what seems to you to be a "dumb" question. They not only will help you learn the names and characteristics of the different hardwoods, but they might explain the various grading and measuring systems used. Most dealers, for example, will explain the difference between kiln-dried (KD) and air-dried (AD) lumber. They probably will show you how the different methods of sawing a log—for example, plain sawing, rift sawing, and quartersawing—affect the way a board looks and its potential use. Seek out the individuals in your area who work with wood and are clearly knowledgeable about it. This kind of information can be a great asset in planning and initiating a range of projects around the house.

PINE: THE RIDICULED WOOD

With few exceptions, I have crafted with most of the common hardwoods and continue to do so on a regular basis. Certain items I craft simply look better and are generally supposed to be made from hardwoods. When I want to build a shelf for my house, however, I always turn to my pile of pine. Pine is unquestionably the wood of choice for home accessories.

For crafting accessories, I normally buy pine that is readily available at my local lumberyard. As a rule, I buy the least expensive grade, but I select the boards very carefully. It is worth noting that I do not use what generally is called *yellow pine*. It tends to split and sliver, normally has very few knots, and is simply a rather drab, unexciting wood. You might want to avoid using it for your projects.

Actually, pine is a rather incredible wood. Shortly, I will provide you with specifics on how to buy it. First, however, I would like to defend this much maligned and ridiculed phenomenon frequently referred to as "It's only pine." Unlike the hardwoods, almost every piece of pine seems to be different. Its grains are unpredictable, and thus fascinating to examine. Pine has large and small, round and oblong knots that are sheer wonderments of detail. It frequently will have a certain red, gray, or brownish hue to it as a result of minerals taken in with water through the root system. You can drive a nail into pine without first drilling a hole. It lends itself to every conceivable type of finish. It smells good and clean, and normally will not make the user sneeze or have an allergic reaction. You literally can make anything out of pine. When you make a serious mistake and ruin a piece, you might have lost some time and effort, but not too much money in material. Also, you frequently can reuse your mistakes. If you are inclined to throwing things in the shop when you become angry or frustrated, pine will not do too much damage to the wall. You can hang an item made of pine on a wall without needing to secure it to studs. Pine cuts well, sands easily, and will hold together with almost any type of glue. In order to get hardwood logs to burn in a fireplace or woodburner, you must start the fire with pine or another softwood. Those who demean this multipurpose wonder of nature are either generally uninformed about wood or are simply snobs. Never apologize for using pine in your projects. Without it, there would be no houses in which to place your projects.

SELECTING PINE FOR PROJECTS

Unlike many other items you purchase, lumber has had a somewhat uniform grading system for many years. Although there remain some inconsistencies, standards regarding the varying qualities of lumber have been in place for many years. There are systems of grading or evaluating both the hardwoods and the softwoods. Each system is different, and each has its own unique symbols and language for varying degrees of quality. The grade a particular board is assigned by a lumber grader generally will determine the final cost to the consumer. As with buying meat or eggs, it can be important to have some working knowledge of lumber grading systems.

Because the focus of this book is pine, it will be important for you to know how pine is graded when you select material for your projects. The following information represents a rather crude compilation of softwood grading and the meaning of the various letters and numbers stamped on boards. References that include more scientifically detailed systems for grading lumber, including hardwoods, are included in the Bibliography.

Select Lumber

Boards that are classified as Select normally are almost perfectly clear. There are usually no knots or other visible flaws in the board. There are generally four grades of select lumber, which are simply identified as: Grade A, B, C, and D. It is very hard for the average person to distinguish between the various grades. Grade A would be defined as the perfect board, while Grade D would have some visible flaws. Grades B and C would fall somewhere between these two extremes. Generally, most Select boards are used for flooring, paneling, finishing, cabinetwork, and trim. As you might guess, Select grades are very expensive and frequently difficult to obtain.

Common Lumber

The second major classification of the softwoods is generally called Common. A board that is graded as Common has too many flaws, knots, or other defects for it to be used for cabinetwork or trim. Boards classified as Common are further broken down by a numbering system.

No. 1. A board that is graded No. 1 Common is usually a rather choice piece. It often will be an almost totally clear board with a few small, but tight, knots. There are seldom any visible signs of sap or mineral coloration. No. 1 generally should have no warps, splits, twists, or decay. These types of flaws are presented in more detail shortly. As a rule, No. 1 is far too expensive for crafting projects. Although cost discourages its use, I also do not buy it because it lacks character. As with the Select grades, it is almost sterile in appearance.

No. 2. As you might guess, No. 2 Common is almost as good as No. 1, but might have some loose knots, a few checks on the end of the board, or some mineral staining. If you are not a lumber grader, I suspect you must take the word of the dealer that a board has been graded No. 2 Common. I have yet to see No. 2 Common in a lumberyard. It really does not seem to be available but, if it does exist, I suspect it is rather expensive.

No. 3. This grade is generally described as a medium-quality board to be used for general construction. It is often quite knotty and has visible defects such as mineral discolorations. There are occasional checks, rotting, and other strange-looking things that you have never seen before in a board. In this grade, a portion of the board often is not usable because of a split or warp. Despite, and yet because of, all that is wrong with No. 3 Common, I view it as the primary medium for the craftsman. To sort through a stack of No. 3 Common is always an exciting experience. The growth process of the tree, its multiple encounters with the elements, and the sheer beauty of a piece of wood confront you as you examine each board. I have found the multiple stacks of No. 3 Common to be almost a natural art gallery—an aesthetic encounter that can be experienced only via some wonderous phenomenon of nature. If you are less inclined to the beauty of the material, remember that No. 3 Common is also considerably less expensive than the other grades.

No. 4. This grade is generally made up of boards that have large knotholes and substantial splits, and is almost useless other than for general construction work. Do not rule this grade out entirely, though. If it is available, you frequently can find enough material for small projects. As you would suspect, this grade should be less expensive than the previous grade.

No. 5. This grade is generally considered to be scrap or waste lumber. I have frequently seen what looks like No. 5 Common, but that has been priced and called No. 3 Common. I cannot ever recall having seen a stack of No. 5 Common in a lumberyard.

As indicated earlier, the foregoing is but a crude and somewhat personal detailing of a rather sophisticated and scientifically based process. To date, it has been adequate to meet my informational needs when approaching the task of buying pine for projects. I would urge you, however, to explore the grading system in more detail as your interest in woodworking develops.

DIMENSIONS AND PRICING OF PINE

In addition to some notion about the grading of softwoods, you also need to realize that the actual width of a board is never the same as its referenced width. The length is almost always accurate. It is the width, unfortunately the thickness too, that gets confusing and requires a bit of memory work.

When boards are cut from a log at the sawmill, they are *rough-cut*. They do not have the smooth finish of the boards you buy at the lumberyard. The sawing process leaves all surfaces and edges of the board very rough. However, rough, unplaned boards always should measure exactly the dimensions stated. For example, a rough, unplaned 1-×-4-inch board should measure exactly 1 inch × 4 inches. This measurement is referred to as its *nominal size*. The lumber you buy is always planed and will not be the exact, or nominal dimensions that it is called. A 1-×-4-inch rough board, after planing, will be ¾ inch × 3½ inches. Table 1-1 presents the nominal (rough-cut) and the true (planed) sizes that you will be buying at a lumberyard. It is important to remember these actual dimensions of the stock when you are planning and laying out your projects.

Although the various board sizes listed in Table 1-1 are not an all-inclusive listing of available materials, they represent the sizes that will be used in the projects in this book. If you commit some of the true dimensions to memory, you will greatly simplify your selection of material at the lumberyard. After a while, however, you will know the various board sizes simply by looking at them.

Familiarity with the various widths also can be helpful when the lumberyard has a limited inventory. For example, if you need 1-×-4 stock for a given project and it is not available, you can always buy 1-×-8 stock

Table 1-1. Dimensions of Lumber.

THICKNESS AND WIDTH (Examples)	
Nominal Size (Rough Cut)	**True Size (Planed)**
1″ × 4″	¾″ × 3 ½″
1″ × 6″	¾″ × 5 ½″
1″ × 8″	¾″ × 7 ¼″
1″ × 10″	¾″ × 9 ¼″
1″ × 12″	¾″ × 11 ¼″
2″ × 4″	1 ½″ × 3 ½″
2″ × 6″	1 ½″ × 5 ½″
2″ × 8″	1 ½″ × 7 ¼″

and ripsaw it. This is not only an efficient way to obtain the needed stock, but it is often economical.

As well as having some knowledge of lumber dimensions and grading before you go to purchase your material, you should have some notion of how lumber prices are figured. Depending upon where you purchase your wood, one of two methods of pricing is generally used. Some lumber dealers sell boards by the lineal foot. A *lineal foot* is literally 12 inches long. The price of a board varies in relation to the width. Thus, a 1-×-4-inch board that is 5 feet long would cost a designated amount based on the lineal-foot price. A 1-×-6-inch board that is 5 feet long would cost more because the lineal-foot price would be higher for a wider board. You probably will discover that dealers who price lumber using this method often have considerably higher prices than lumberyard dealers who deal in volume and use a different pricing method. On occasion, however, you might only need one board and will find that buying it at a store which sells by the lineal foot is quick and easy.

Lumber dealers or distributors normally sell lumber by the board foot. A *board foot* of lumber is equal to the width (in inches) times the thickness (in inches) times the length (in feet) divided by 12. A simpler definition is that a board foot is 1 square foot of lumber that is 1 inch thick. Incidentally, when measuring the board to compute its cost, the lumber dealer uses the nominal size and not the true size of the board. The cost of having the board planed is figured into the board-foot price. An example of how to figure the board feet in a piece of pine lumber follows:

Board to be purchased is: 1″ (thick) × 6″ (wide) × 12′ (long)

$$\frac{\text{Thickness (inches)} \times \text{Width (inches)} \times \text{Length (feet)}}{12} = 1 \text{ board foot}$$

$$\frac{1″ \text{ (thickness)} \times 6″ \text{ (width)} \times 6′ \text{ (length)}}{12} = \frac{72}{12} = 6 \text{ board feet}$$

After making these calculations, the lumber dealer would check the current price per board foot for the grade and dimensions of the board selected. Since lumber dealers and their suppliers deal in terms of thousands of board feet, the prices are calculated in the thousands. To take the example one more step, your lumber dealer will tell you that your 1-×-6 board that is 12 feet long will cost $.2760 per board foot. Since you know you have 12 board feet in your piece of lumber, simple multiplication will tell you the cost of the board.

$$\begin{array}{rl}
\$\ .2760 & \text{price per board foot} \\
\times\quad 12 & \text{number of board feet in } 1'' \times 6'' \times 12' \text{ piece} \\
\hline
\$3.31 & \text{the cost of your board}
\end{array}$$

Although all these measurements and calculations are done for you at the lumberyard, it is worth being knowledgeable about the process. More often than not, you will find yourself selecting boards based on project need and appearance, rather than board feet. As you will discover the more you engage in woodworking, inches and fractions of an inch will be the kind of measuring in which you will need to develop some skill.

SHOPPING FOR PINE

Because you should have sufficient background information about lumber, I will address the actual shopping process for wood. Obviously, before you start for the lumberyard, you should have some idea of what you are going to make. You can focus or even accelerate this decision by reviewing, in detail, some of the projects in this book. Let us assume, for purposes of discussion, that you have decided to make the Plate Shelf. After measuring the area where you plan to hang the shelf, you decide it should be 24 inches long and at least 5 inches wide. Following some pencil and paper work with your design, patterns, and ruler, you decide you will need a 1-×-6 board that is 6 feet long. Let us further assume that you will purchase your lumber at your local lumberyard.

On occasion as you enter the world of a lumber dealer, you will find yourself being "helped" by someone who assumes you are stupid. I suspect this situation might be especially true for women entering this traditionally male domain. In addition to having good information about the material you want, you should bring along a tape measure. Indicate to the person waiting on you what you need and that you would like to select the material yourself. Some lumberyards discourage customers from entering areas where personal injury could result. Frequently, however, they will permit access to the lumber storage areas if you are accompanied by an employee.

Lumber is usually stacked according to grade, width, and length. Hopefully, an employee will lead you to an area where you will see stacks of 1 × 4s, 1 × 6s, and 1 × 8s, all No. 3 Common pine. Generally you also will find wider stock in the same grade stacked nearby. Using your tape measure, check the width and length of some of the boards. This measuring process is very helpful during your initial visits to the lumberyard. It helps to familiarize yourself with the various widths and lengths of the available material. After a while, you will be able to identify width and even length by simply looking at a board. If you are like me, length is often something of a problem. I need to measure the length of a board when I buy lumber. On occasion, I can approximate length, but I always measure to be certain. Actually, this is probably a good practice in relation to the eventual cost of the board. Mistakes are made, especially in length of boards.

To continue with our lumber shopping example, find a stack of 1-×-6 No. 3 Common pine. Remember that the true dimensions of a 1-×-6 board are actually ¾ inch × 5½ inches. In selecting boards, you will need to pull off each board and look at both sides and the edges. It is important to remember that you are looking at No. 3 Common, so expect some flaws. Some of the visual flaws you will want in the board, but others you should avoid. If the board is badly warped (Fig. 1-1), leave it. Sometimes you can see the warp as you look over the entire flat surface of the board. I often pick the board up and sight the length from one end to the other end. A very slight warp might be acceptable, especially if the board has other good qualities, for example, beautiful, tight knots. Make a judgment based on the project you will be making.

Other flaws you should look for are cracks or what sometimes amount to actual splits in the board (Fig. 1-2). You need to examine the entire length of the board, on both sides, for splits. Cracks in the surface or splits can, at times, be very difficult to see. Sometimes they will run only for a short distance in the board. At other times, they will penetrate the entire length of the board. What happens is that when you cut your 24-inch-long piece for the shelf top, you suddenly discover that you have two splintered 24-inch pieces. The board literally breaks into two pieces along the split.

Sap also can be a problem that you need to be aware of as you look over the boards. Boards that seem unusually heavy in relation to other boards of the same length and width frequently are loaded with sap. Leave them because they are useless for making projects. These sap-laden boards often are tan to brown in color. Often they appear to be wet and even glossy in appearance. Many boards will have small pockets in them with sap bleeding out of them. If there are not too many of these pockets, portions of the board might be acceptable. It is important to remember that finishes will not take or hold over sap. Also, you do not want a pocket of sap that will continue to drain or bleed on a finished project. There is no effective way to cover sap and keep it from seeping. It is best to leave these boards on the stack.

Knots are another major consideration in your selection process. Check knots to be certain that they are tight. Knots that have a black circle around their outer edges are often the kind that will fall out or pop out as you work on the board. A few knots that are loose or even a few knotholes in a board might be acceptable. Look at the board in terms of how much material remains usable. The kind of knots that you want in the board are generally reddish in color and are very tight. They appear to be an integral part of the wood. Size is not necessarily a factor, although sometimes the centers of larger, tight

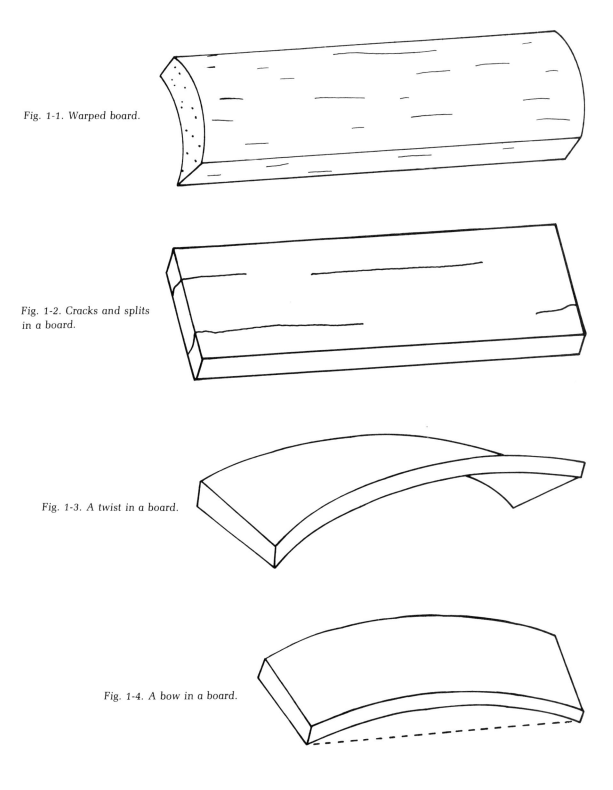

Fig. 1-1. Warped board.

Fig. 1-2. Cracks and splits
in a board.

Fig. 1-3. A twist in a board.

Fig. 1-4. A bow in a board.

knots tend to partially break out. If they break out while you are working on the board, you can patch them easily with wood putty. Many of the larger knots are highly desirable for crafting, and simply require a bit more sanding during the finishing process. With a few exceptions, most good knots can be sawed through when necessary. It is preferable, however, to lay out your project in such a way that you avoid cutting through the knots.

One final word on the matter of knots. If you plan to do tole painting on your finished projects, you would be wise to avoid knots altogether. They tend to distract from the painted design and, often, are difficult to paint on. Most tole painters prefer perfectly clear boards.

Quite frequently as you examine pine boards, you will notice a narrow, rather long, reddish brown streak in the surface. Poke it with your fingernail; it very well might be rot. Sometimes the rot is sufficiently hard and will add to the overall attractiveness of the board. When it is soft or chips out, you might want to leave the board unless it is a rather small amount of surface. You frequently will work around some small areas of rot when you are laying out the project on the board.

For a host of reasons, boards sometimes will have a twist in them (Fig. 1-3). Others, if you examine them carefully, will be bowed (Fig. 1-4). A slight twist or minor bow might be acceptable if the board has other redeeming qualities. On the other hand, if the problem seems severe, I would leave the board. These types of flaws often are caused by faulty drying of the lumber. They can present a real hazard when they are being cut on a radial arm or table saw.

Frequently you will notice that a portion of a pine board will have a grey color to it. It almost looks as if it were stained or painted grey. Normally, the grey color is from minerals taken in with the water through the root system of the tree. I think this greying enhances the beauty of a board, but it can present problems if you plan to stain your project. If you use a dark stain, the grey portions of the board will become almost black. A light stain or a natural finish is generally not affected by the greying. Whether you take a board with mineral staining it it is a matter of personal taste. Incidentally, tole painters tend to avoid boards having mineral stains.

Another thing you should always do as you examine boards is to check the actual width and thickness of the board. Sometimes a board will be overplaned and be too thin. On occasion, the width also might be wrong as a result of the milling process. When in doubt, measure.

A final reminder from my own experience. You probably will need to haul your lumber in a car, so do not buy anything you cannot haul. Hauling lumber can be very dangerous and must be planned for ahead of time. I sometimes will cut a long board into two pieces in relation to the project I plan to make. Either carry a hand saw in the car or ask the lumberyard to cut the board for you. If material will extend behind the car, find a red flag and tie it on the board. Think safety.

Chapter 2

Tools and Crafting Supplies

Although many of the projects presented in this volume have been designed to be made with a few hand and small power tools, some can be crafted more easily with large, floor-model power tools. Obviously, the larger floor-model tools will greatly simplify making all of the projects. In my own crafting, I use an assortment of small power tools, hand tools, and some larger floor-model power tools. This is not to suggest that you must have an array of power tools to undertake the various projects presented in this book. Rather, it is intended to suggest the range and diversity of tools that can be used in making small projects from pine. Most of the tools required are usually found in most households. Those that are not can be purchased with a minimal investment.

In addition to a diversity of tools, the various projects in this book lend themselves to varying levels of skill. Most of the projects are within the reach of the beginning woodworker who has limited or no experience with tools. If you will be making projects for the first time, it would be wise to use small power and hand tools initially. This approach not only minimizes your investment, it also eliminates the need to familiarize yourself with the more dangerous, complex, and expensive floor-model power tools. As you will discover in the brief overview of tools, there are numerous methods and tools the beginner can use. Although the woodworking process might be slower when hand and small power tools are used, it is just as effective and, in many ways, more fun.

It is a good practice to shop around at the various hardware stores in your community. This process not only helps you to understand what kinds of tools are available, it also gives you some sense of their prices. Very often the store employees are willing to provide additional information about the various tools they stock. It is also worth noting the range of tool accessories available in your local stores, since all woodworking tools usually require some type of accessory, ranging from a bit to a blade.

Mail-order catalogs provided by woodworking suppliers also are helpful in learning about tools and their various accessories. In addition to detailed descriptions of the various tools, they often provide information on how the tool can be used and what accessories are best. Catalogs also give you a good idea of the prices of the various tools and their accessories. A listing of some mail-order suppliers is provided in the Appendix.

If you already have a variety of tools and accessories, the projects in this book should be equally challenging. The various projects will afford you the opportunity to develop additional skills with your tools but, more importantly, allow you to make some very different projects. You might want to produce any number of the projects in quantity to sell at local shows. All of the project designs have been sold successfully at a wide range of craft shows, in addition to gift shops. It is an excellent way to support your woodworking hobby or to make some extra money.

Because the process of woodworking is a series of related functions, it seems appropriate to briefly discuss tools in this framework. Although various accessories can enable a tool to have a number of functions, most tools have but one function. It is these primary woodworking functions and the tools that will accomplish them that are our concern. Although the listing of tools is by no means complete, it is sufficient to enable you to make the various projects presented in Chapter 3. Also note that there are additional functions to the woodworking process not mentioned here. Those that are described result in a process that will facilitate the making of small pine projects.

THE SAFETY FUNCTION

The safety function must overshadow all subsequent functions and the total woodworking process. The matter of safety cannot be overstressed. Never use any tool, whether hand or power, until you have a complete understanding of how the tool works and what hazards it presents to you. Carefully study the owner's manual that accompanies each tool, especially power tools. In the woodworking process, you are working with tools that are driving extremely sharp pieces of steel at high speeds. The potential for serious injury is always present. It is a good practice to develop a listing of medical specialists that you can use in the event of injury. I have a listing of specialists that is prominently displayed by the telephone in case a shop accident should occur. Although I have never had reason to call on this medical expertise, I know how to reach them in the event of an accident. The displayed listing of names and their specialties also has a certain chilling effect that continually reminds me of safety.

Whenever you are using tools, you should use protective devices. Always wear a face mask or safety glasses when you are working with tools. Ear plugs or other devices to protect the ears from the high-pitched noises of power tools should be mandatory in your shop. Most of these safety devices are readily available at local hardware or discount stores. Purchase them before you start any woodworking activities. Incidentally, I often wear leather gloves when I am working with small, sharp hand tools.

Also in my shop, I have bright red signs with the word *Danger* on them placed over every power tool. Also, various signs that employ some vulgarity remind me of safety. You will find that these kinds of practices tend to keep issues of safety paramount in your shop. I also have several commercial fire extinguishers in the shop.

Although it is not my intention to terrify you before you even begin making your projects, it is my hope that you deal realistically with matters of safety. Shop injuries are generally the result of carelessness with tools. Think and practice safety. It makes woodworking a lot more fun and certainly less painful.

THE MEASURING FUNCTION

Although measuring is one of the least dramatic functions in woodworking, it is clearly one of the most critical. Since measuring procedures are so obvious and attainable, it is easy to take them for granted. As a result, it is easy to become careless and make basic errors. Most problems in making anything from wood are the result of careless measuring. Incidentally, as you plan for the measuring function, do not rule out the use of the metric system. It is effective and very simple to use.

As I suggested in the discussion on selecting pine, a tape measure is almost mandatory. You need the capability to measure the length of boards when you are selecting them as well as when you are laying out a piece to cut. A wide range of compact tapes is available that will permit you to measure lengths up to 25 feet or more. They are large enough to use in a lumberyard, but compact enough to use in a shop. Be certain the tape has graduations of at least $\frac{1}{16}$ inch marked on its surface. Although you might not need these smaller fractions often, they are worth having should an occasion for their use arise.

You also should have a couple of standard rulers with clean, sharp edges. I have found a 36-foot aluminum ruler to be useful in laying out projects. A 12-inch metal ruler with a rubber backing is also worth having around. On smaller projects, I tend to rely exclusively on the smaller 12-inch ruler. If it has a rubber backing, this type of ruler can be used for cutting glass and other tasks related to the projects. You should purchase a metal ruler rather than a wood one. Metal rulers hold their sharp edges, are graduated more accurately, and are less prone to breaking.

A try square is also useful in making the projects. Although you can make a try square easily, you might prefer to buy one. Another excellent device is a combination square. You need something that can correctly make a straight, vertical line from the edge of boards. This function becomes critical if you are sawing your boards with a hand or small electric saber saw. You need to have a good, straight line to follow when cutting. Combination squares enable you to make straight lines. They have other functions but, for the projects in this book, their use is limited to layout work. If you prefer a larger square for use in home remodeling as well as for the projects, you might want to consider purchasing a steel square.

There is an assortment of other clever and very useful devices for measuring that you might want to consider. For example, a school compass is an effective and inexpensive device for measuring circles for projects. When it is time to hang a shelf, you might want to purchase a small torpedo level (Fig. 2-1). These small levels, along with their larger counterparts, can be extremely useful in the woodworking process. There are all types of measuring devices that you can use for a variety of functions around the house. You will find them very helpful both in the shop and for hanging the various projects you make.

THE SAWING FUNCTION

The sawing function can be effectively accomplished with an array of tools. Although speed and accuracy are involved in sawing, the basic issue is whether you want to do it by hand or with a power tool. Since pine cuts considerably easier than the hardwoods, the use of hand tools is a very real option. You might be limited when you are cutting some of the detailed scrollwork on a few designs, but you can make most projects using various handsaws.

Handsaws

There are any number of handsaws available that can do your sawing of straight cuts, curves, and even some details. Many handsaws also can make cuts other than what they were designed to do. For example, a metal cutting hacksaw can be used to make a straight cut in pine. The hacksaw is an excellent all-around tool to have available for a range of household projects. Other general-purpose saws that are relatively inexpensive are utility saws. These types of saws generally have a number of blades and can be used for straight cuts as well as curves. They also are effective for cutting internal holes in a project. As a rule, if a particular type of handsaw can do the job at hand, without danger to you, why not use it. Do not abuse the tool, but use it to accomplish the necessary task.

Better quality and more effective handsaws are available for either crosscut sawing or ripsawing. Each type of cut requires a different type of handsaw, for example a crosscut saw or a standard ripsaw. Many households seem to have one or both of these types of saws around. They are extremely effective for working with pine and great fun to use.

Other handsaws that you might want to consider are the miter saw for

Fig. 2-1. Torpedo level (courtesy of Stanley Tools).

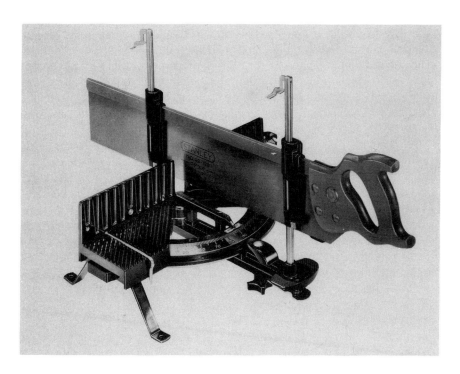

Fig. 2-2. Professional miter box (courtesy of Stanley Tools).

straight cuts and the coping saw for curves. The miter saw, especially when used with a hand-made miter box, is effective for both straight and mitered cuts. Of course, you might have a standard professional miter box (Fig. 2-2). Although miter saws are restricted in terms of the width they can cut, they can perform many sawing functions for a range of projects. The small coping saw, although initially difficult to use, can be extremely effective for cutting curves, especially in pine. Both the coping saw and replacement blades are inexpensive. As with any tool, you will find some practice is necessary for you to become an effective user of the coping saw.

A relatively new, at least to this country, type of saw on the market is the Japanese handsaw. These saws are available in a range of styles to make different cuts. Although somewhat expensive, they are extremely effective for a handsaw. A number of mail-order suppliers listed in the Appendix stock Japanese saws, in addition to the more traditional ones discussed earlier.

Power Saws

A preferable way to perform the various sawing functions for the projects is to use a saber saw. A wide variety of these excellent and highly versatile small power tools are on the market. Basically, the saber saw is a hand-held power jigsaw that offers immense versatility to the crafter. Depending upon the type of blade used, you can make straight cuts, circles, angles, or any combination of cuts with relative ease. Although safety should be a primary consideration in the use of any tool, the sabersaw is much less dangerous than many other kinds of power saws.

If you do not have a saber saw you can purchase an adequate tool at your local hardware store or through a mail-order supplier. Frequently, through comparative shopping, you can purchase a much better tool for less money from a mail-order supplier. You will find that commercial-grade tools can be purchased often for little more than the standard hobbyist's tool. You might want to buy one that comes with an edge guide for making straight cuts. This device greatly increases the capabilities of the tool.

A major factor in the use of the saber saw is the type of blade that is used. You will be somewhat overwhelmed by the variety of blades on the market. I generally purchase blades designed for fine cuts or scroll sawing. Usually, blades are described by their length and the number of teeth per inch. I usually use a blade that is about 5 inches long and has 20 teeth per inch. The more teeth per inch a blade has, the smoother the cut. The reason I use the finer cutting blades is that, in addition to being more versatile in the types of cuts you can make, they also leave the wood edges relatively smooth, thus eliminating the need for a lot of extra sanding.

Two other types of power saws that can be useful are the hand circular saw and the electric miter saw. The hand circular saw is a tool often found around the house of someone who has done remodeling. This type of saw is available in a range of blade diameters. It can be very effective for making straight cuts on pine of varying thicknesses. The power miter saw is an extremely effective tool for making either straight or miter cuts. It is a superb tool for making any kind of mitered frames. As with any power saw, use these tools only after you have carefully studied the safety procedures in the owner's manual.

If you are inclined to the larger floor-model power saws, a radial arm or table saw is highly effective. These tools are not mandatory to any of the projects in this book. They do, however, greatly speed up the crafting process. With a circular saw, these tools can quickly perform all of your crosscutting and ripping for a range of projects. Also, you can use both tools for other types of sawing. In recent years, the radial arm saw has become very popular with the homeowner, do-it-yourself woodworker. The standard table saw remains the tool of choice of the professional woodworker. If you are planning to make crafts to sell at local shows, you definitely should consider buying one of these larger saws. As an aside, the circular saw blade was invented by a woman. Sister Tabitha Babbitt, a Shaker, invented it in about 1810. The circular saw blade represents one of the major contributions to woodworking.

Another floor-model tool that offers great versatility to the crafter is the band saw. In addition to making cross cuts, this tool is ideal for ripping stock and resawing it. I frequently resaw standard ¾-inch-thick pine into ½-inch-thick material for use with projects. Generally, for resawing stock, you want to use a ½-inch-wide blade.

A related floor-model tool that can clean up the sawed surface or edges of a board is a jointer (Fig. 2-3). If you are developing a shop or considering making items for sale, you also might want to purchase a small planer. The planer will permit you to reduce the thickness of your boards very quickly

and to exact dimensions. To minimize waste, after resawing a board on the band saw, I plane the cut surface. Although both jointers and planers are expensive, they are tools you might want to consider if you decide to get serious about woodworking. They are, however, not necessary to do the projects presented in this book.

The band saw also offers excellent capability for detailed scrollwork. You can make many decorative cuts using a ⅛-inch or ¼-inch-wide blade on a band saw. Using a self-made jig, I also cut large round pieces on the band saw. It is an ideal circle cutter when round pieces are needed for decorative or functional projects. Although the band saw is not mandatory for any of the projects in this book, it is one of the most useful tools in the shop. If you are planning to develop a shop someday, by all means include a band saw among your tools.

If you have one of the floor-model power jigsaws, you can make many of the projects in this book with relative ease. In recent years, a series of large jig or scroll saws using a range of new technologies have become available. The jig or large scroll saw is ideal for making decorative detail, but it is limited to this function. You still need another tool to make crosscuts and rips in boards. These larger tools are expensive but, again, are an excellent addition to any shop. If you are planning to make the projects in quantity, you might want to consider one of these larger floor-model scroll saws. They are available in a wide range of styles and prices.

Although this listing of tools is but a sampling, it should indicate that you can perform the sawing function with a diversity of tools. The way you accomplish the various sawing functions required by the projects will very much depend upon your ability and willingness to purchase tools. Fortunately, many households already have several of the tools just described. Your immediate problem might simply be learning how to use your tools effectively and safely.

THE DRILLING FUNCTION

As with the sawing function, the process of drilling the various required holes can be accomplished with a variety of tools and accessories. In addition to the primary drilling tool, you can use a wide variety of bits for the projects. By way of accuracy, in woodworking, the drilling function is generally called *boring*. It seems, however, that most people tend to refer to making holes in anything as a process of drilling rather than boring.

Hand Tools

If you are inclined to use hand tools, the brace and bit are effective to achieve the drilling function. This hand-held tool is a delight for making holes. Although the user must provide the power, the brace and bit are extremely accurate and relatively easy to use. With this combination, you can generate large, interesting shavings that give you a real sense of working with wood. Unless you already have a brace and an assortment of bits, they can be rather costly. If you buy bits, be certain you purchase the kind required for a brace. Incidentally, never use a wood bit designed for a brace in a power drill. These bits are not designed or manufactured to function at the high speeds generated by electric drills.

The brace, like many other tools, sometimes can be found at flea markets or auctions. If you should find a used one, check to be certain that the chuck (the part that holds the bit) is all there and working. If it works, you might have solved your drilling problems with an effective and enjoyable tool. You

Fig. 2-4. Yankee drill (courtesy of Stanley Tools).

will never get into mass production with a brace and bit, but you certainly will have a good time and make some fine projects.

For making small holes for starting screws, a good device to use is a yankee drill (Fig. 2-4). This tool also is hand-powered, but is very effective for making small holes. Be sure to use only drill points specifically designed for the tool (Fig. 2-5). Another type of small hand drill, which can use standard high-speed steel bits, is also very effective (Fig. 2-6). You need a drilling capacity for making small holes for a number of projects. These types of tools are almost mandatory if you do not have an electric drill.

Hand Power Drills

The hand power drill is probably the one tool most people are likely to own.

Fig. 2-5. Drill points (courtesy of Stanley Tools).

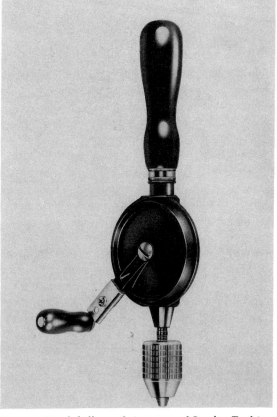

Fig. 2-6. Hand drill: crank (courtesy of Stanley Tools).

As with saber saws, the brands and types of power drills available are numerous. Many drills are designed, built, and priced for the homeowner/hobbyist market.

Be certain to check the various consumer reports and sources of shopper information if you find it necessary to buy a drill. Also check the catalogs of mail-order suppliers before you purchase a tool locally. Very often you can buy a commercial-grade tool for not much more than the hobbyist type. As a rule, the commercial tools have superior electrical components and bearings. They are generally built and designed for continuous use, whereas the hobbyist tool can be overused easily. If you are planning to buy tools, spend a few dollars more and purchase those designed for commercial or industrial use. You will be more than satisfied with both the quality and longevity of the tool.

Hand electric drills are generally referred to as ½-inch, ⅜-inch, or ¼-inch tools. These designations have to do with a number of factors. Primarily, they refer to the size of the chuck that holds the bit. Although bits might be almost any diameter, the ends that are held in the chuck are usually ½ inch, ⅜ inch, or ¼ inch. You must buy your bits in relation to the diameter your drill chuck will accommodate. The actual speed of the drill or bit also varies according to these designations. For example, a ¼-inch drill usually has a speed ranging from 1,600 to 2,800 revolutions per minute. These smaller drills generally revolve faster and have less power than the larger ones. If you need to buy a drill, you would be wise to consider purchasing a ⅜-inch one. They are more powerful and also allow you to use a greater variety of bits.

Another feature of hand power drills is *variable speed*. This feature allows you to control the speed of the drill bit by varying the amount of finger pressure on the trigger. Normally, the drill rotates clockwise. In addition to the variable speed, some drills have a reversing capacity. By simply pushing a switch on the tool, the bit will rotate counterclockwise. This is a very useful feature for extracting stuck bits and for removing screws.

Although a hand power drill is adequate for making the various projects in this book, you might have or prefer a floor-model drill press. As you might guess, these larger tools are considerably more powerful and enable more accurate drilling to be done. They are also substantially more expensive. A drill press can be an indispensable tool once you have used one. If you already own a drill press, it will serve you well in making the various projects in this book. There is no need, however, to purchase one for making projects from pine. A hand power drill, properly used and with appropriate bits, can accomplish the drilling tasks for all the projects. One distinct advantage of the drill press is that you are able to use a wide variety of accessories that the smaller tools cannot handle or accommodate.

One final type of hand power drill needs to be mentioned: the air-drive or pneumatic drills. In recent years, a variety of reasonably priced air tools have become available. They generally outlast and outperform electric tools. The only significant drawback with pneumatic tools is that you also need an air compressor. However, small 1-horsepower air compressors are becoming increasingly popular with homeowners. They provide sufficient air pressure for automotive uses, painting, and of course, pneumatic tools. I find my air compressor to be indispensable for blowing dust off pieces prior to finishing. They are also very effective for blowing dust from clothing. You might want to examine some of the available pneumatic tools if you already have an air compressor.

Bits

Major factors in the drilling function are the actual drills or bits that are required by the various tools. Here again, there is an almost overwhelming variety of drills, bits, and drilling accessories on the market. For making the various projects in this book, you need only a few basic bits. Although the diameter required might vary among projects, the type of bits necessary are essentially the same. Before you buy bits, you should examine the various mail-order catalogs that are available. Many companies sell commercial bits that are considerably less expensive than bits available at a local store. They also have a greater selection of quality wood bits.

Bits used primarily for metalworking are helpful in a number of the projects in this book (Fig. 2-7). Normally these bits are called *high-speed steel bits* and are available in a range of diameters and lengths. Extra-long bits, often called *aircraft bits,* are also readily available. I frequently use this type of bit to drill holes of ¼ inch diameter and less. A ⅜- or ¼-inch-diameter bit is excellent for drilling holes to receive a saber saw blade when you are making an internal cut in a project. As you will discover in the projects, the larger high-speed bits also can be very useful.

One problem with high-speed steel bits is that they tend to *skate*, or run around on the surface of a board. Their points are dull because they are not designed for immediate penetration. Because they are designed for use in metal, their points are rounded. You can eliminate this surface skating by making a slight indentation in the wood surface where you will drill the hole. When you need to use these type of bits with a project design, I will indicate specific sizes.

Spade bits, unlike high-speed bits, are designed for use in wood (Fig. 2-8). They are, however, available only in limited diameters. Although spade bits are by no means the most effective wood bore, you might want to use them because of price and availability. You frequently can find spade bits in local discount stores. One problem with spade bits is that they tend to slap the wood as you drill into the board. You will discover that, if you are not careful while drilling, the hole diameter will be a little larger than planned. For some projects, this lack of tolerance is usually not a problem. On other projects, you definitely will need more accuracy when you are drilling holes. Another advantage of the spade bit is that it can be resharpened easily with a whetstone or file. To keep your costs down, you might want to purchase some of these bits.

An excellent, but somewhat more expensive, bit is the power bore bit (Fig. 2-9). This type of bit has an extra long point for precise and immediate

Fig. 2-7. High-speed steel bit (courtesy of Vermont American Tool Co.).

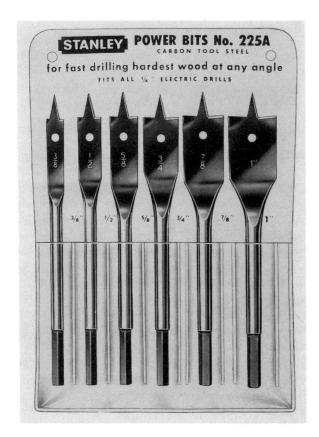

Fig. 2-8. Spade bits (courtesy of Stanley Tools).

penetration into the board's surface. The bit is designed to drill holes rapidly and cleanly, especially in soft wood. Power bores and spade bits both have a ¼-inch-diameter shank that can be held in either a hand drill or a drill press. The power bore is available in diameters from ⅜ to 1 inch. I have used these bits over the years in crafting pine and have found them very effective. They would be an excellent choice to accomplish the drilling functions on the various projects.

No doubt the best all-around wood bit is the brad-point bit (Fig. 2-10). Some users refer to this bit as a *spur bit*. The center of the bit has a small, sharp spear that quickly penetrates the board's surface and holds the bit in place. The bit has two sharp spurs that do the actual cutting in the wood. The bit is spiral so it enters the wood easily and also ejects the wood shavings.

The brad point is designed to work equally well in hard or soft woods. As with the other wood bits, brad points generally are available with diameters ranging from ¼ to 1 inch. The bits often are sold in sets, but they can be purchased individually. Most brad-point bits are designed to fit a ¼-inch drill chuck. You might want to examine the various mail-order catalogs for these bits. They are generally available to most tool suppliers at rather competitive prices. If you need to buy bits for the projects, I would recommend the brad points. Incidentally, you also can sharpen the brad points.

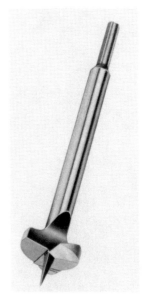

Fig. 2-9. Power bore bit (courtesy of Stanley Tools).

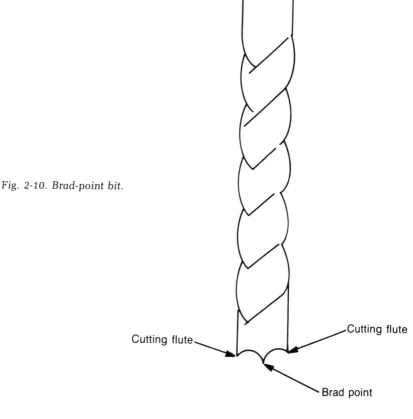

Fig. 2-10. Brad-point bit.

Cutting flute

Cutting flute

Brad point

Fig. 2-11. Forstner bit (courtesy of Leichtung, Inc.).

In recent years, another superb wood bit has become available in this country. The forstner bit has , until recently, been used primarily by European woodworkers (Fig. 2-11). These bits are designed to drill into wood at angles, into end grain, and even into knots. They are highly versatile and, unlike other wood bits, leave a flat-bottomed drill hole. The bit is extremely accurate, but can be somewhat difficult to align over a small mark on the board's surface. The center point of the forstner is very short. These bits are now available in diameters ranging from ¼ inch to 2 inches. If you can purchase quality forstners at a reasonable price, you might want to consider them for your drilling tasks.

A final bit to consider is the multispur machine bit (Fig. 2-12). Since these bits are generally manufactured with ½-inch-diameter shanks, they are usually limited to use on a drill press. They are, however, frequently used on a lathe. Multispur bits are fast cutting and can make a hole with a great deal of accuracy. You also can drill to a greater depth with the multispur than with other wood bits. Whenever you are using this type of bit, you must reduce the speed of the drill, you also should clamp the wood being drilled onto the drill press. Although expensive, multispur bits are long-lasting and can be sharpened easily. They are available in diameters of ½ inch to 2½ inches.

Most mail-order tool suppliers carry a range of these bits. If you have a drill press, you might want to consider using these bits for your projects.

Drilling Accessories

In the context of the drilling function, a number of important drilling accessories also should be mentioned. One accessory that you might want to use is a plug cutter (Fig. 2-13). These small cutters can be used on both a hand drill or a floor drill press. Either way, be sure to clamp the wood. You can use plug cutters to make plugs of varying diameters to fill screw holes. You also can use them to cut plugs for decorative inlay work. You might prefer to buy commercial plugs, which are available from a number of suppliers, and eliminate the expense of buying a cutter. I have found the plug cutters to be an effective way of making my own plugs for projects. They allow you to cut plugs of the particular type of wood needed. Plug cutters are available in a range of diameters from ¼ to ⅝ inch.

Some type of countersink, to be used on either a hand drill or drill press, can be useful in making projects (Fig. 2-14). While countersinks are for preparing screw holes, they also can be used to make hanging holes on shelf-support brackets. A more useful, but also more costly, way to countersink and drill at the same time, is to purchase a drill and countersink set. I frequently use the countersink drill to make holes in exposed surfaces of accessories that are to be hung on a nail. It is a quick and efficient way to make a finished-looking nail hole through a project. Some of these and other uses of these devices will become more apparent in the context of the projects.

Another useful device that is especially effective with pine is the hole saw. Hole saws are available in a range of diameters and can be used on either a hand drill or large drill press. For making small holes for a number of projects, a hole saw can be rather effective. When you are using these kind of devices, you should always clamp the board being drilled. Frequently, the saw will grab an unclamped board and hurl it at the user.

A final drilling accessory that you might want to consider using with some projects is a circle cutter (Fig. 2-15). This device requires a drill press. Depending upon the size of circle cutter you purchase, you can cut circles to a diameter of about 8½ inches. It is imperative that you clamp the wood firmly to the drill press table when you use a circle cutter. The circle cutter is especially effective for use with pine. If you have a drill press, you might want to purchase a circle cutter for use with some of the projects.

Although there are numerous other devices available to assist you in making projects, the foregoing should provide you with an informed overview of some of the more useful ones. As you explore hardware stores and mail-order tool catalogs, you will discover there is an almost endless array of different accessories and bits to assist you in the drilling function.

THE ROUTING FUNCTION

Although this function is more appropriately called a *shaping* function, routing is more descriptive of how best to perform certain project tasks. The router

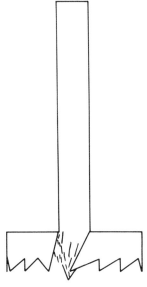

Fig. 2-12. Multispur bit.

Fig. 2-13. Plug cutter (courtesy of Stanley Tools).

Fig. 2-14. Countersink
(courtesy of Stanley Tools).

Fig. 2-15. Circle cutter
(courtesy of Stanley Tools).

is the tool of choice for accomplishing a range of shaping functions for most, if not all of the projects in this book. This is not to rule out the use of a floor-model shaper. If you are planning to equip your shop for more sophisticated and production woodworking, a shaper is almost imperative. It is more likely, however, that a router is the tool most homeowners and hobbyists would own and have some experience using.

The router is the ideal tool for many necessary tasks in most of the pine projects. In fact, if so desired, you can use the router on all the larger projects. If you are inclined to use hand tools exclusively, however, you might want to consider using either a block plane or a surfoam pocket plane. Both of these tools are very effective and affordable. Although they have only limited functions, for example, edge planing, they can be useful in making the projects.

In making the various projects, you will find a table-mounted router to be especially useful. When it is mounted under a table, a router can perform many functions that it cannot when hand held. If you have a router but not a table, you would be well advised to either make one or purchase one of the many commercial tables available. They are well worth having to increase the versatility of this multipurpose tool and to make the crafting of projects easier. You will find a router almost mandatory for much of the detail work on the pine projects.

Usually a router that is rated as 1 horsepower is more than adequate for making the various projects. Routers of this size generally have a ¼-inch collet to hold the various router bits. Most router bits are available with a ¼-inch-diameter shank that can be held in the ¼-inch collet. Although router bits

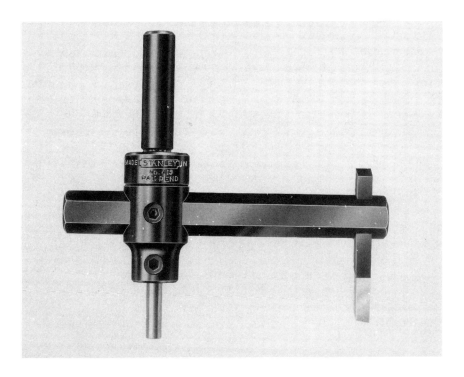

are also available with ⅜- and ½-inch-diameter shanks, these larger bits generally are designed for more powerful routers. It would be to your advantage to shop the various mail-order supply catalogs if you need to buy a router or bits. There is a wide range of high-quality tools now available through mail-order suppliers.

In addition to a table for mounting your router, you will need a number of specific router bits for some of the projects. Router bits are available in either high-speed steel, carbide tips, or solid carbide. Although carbide bits outlast the high-speed steel bits, they are also considerably more expensive. In selecting bits, you need to consider how often you will use them. If you will use them only occasionally you might prefer the less expensive high-speed steel over the carbide. One advantage of high-speed steel is that it can be resharpened easily on a standard grinding stone. Carbide bits require special stones for sharpening. Although some of my bits are carbide, I usually buy the high-speed steel ones and sharpen them myself. For working with pine, the high-speed bits are more than adequate. You will need to clean your bits more frequently when you are working with pine. The sap tends to collect rather quickly on the bit. Kerosene or a commercial solvent for cleaning bits is usually recommended for removing sap.

Although there are many different styles and sizes of router bits available, only a few different bits are necessary for making the pine projects. When a project requires the routing function, I indicate the type and approximate size of bit that works best for me. The following bits are some of the ones that I use most frequently.

The ⅜-inch or ½-inch round-over bit is used primarily for routing the edges of projects (Fig. 2-16). It probably is the most commonly used router bit for rounding over the edges of the various parts of a project. The ⅜-inch cove bit is an excellent alternative for routing edges on project components (Fig. 2-17). Although somewhat more decorative than a round-over bit, it gives edges a more formal appearance. The rabbeting bit, usually only available in a ⅜-inch diameter, is used primarily for mirror or picture frames (Fig. 2-18). It allows you to cut a rabbet or recessed area in a frame where either the mirror glass, picture, or frame glass is placed. A ⅜-inch-diameter V-groove router bit is indispensable for making plate shelves (Fig. 2-19). The V-groove, along with a number of other types of bits, can be used to make a recess in the top surface of a plate shelf. The edge of the plates rest in the groove so they do not slide off the shelf surface.

For a more decorative edging on shelves and other projects, a roman ogee bit is very effective (Fig. 2-20). Some woodworkers tend to use the roman ogee almost exclusively on the edges of their projects. The chamfer bit also can be used to give an interesting effect to an edge (Fig. 2-21). It makes a clean, sharp taper on the edges of boards.

A multipurpose router bit is the ¼-inch straight bit (Fig. 2-22). The larger ¾-inch-diameter straight or mortising bit is used less frequently than its smaller counterparts (Fig. 2-23). You will need one, however, for one very interesting project.

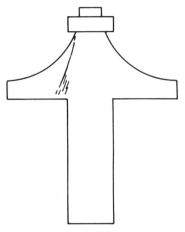

Fig. 2-16. Round-over router bit.

Fig. 2-19. V-groove router bit.

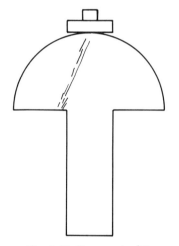

Fig. 2-17. Cove router bit.

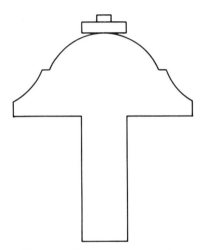

Fig. 2-20. Roman ogee router bit.

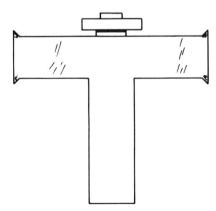

Fig. 2-18. Rabbeting router bit.

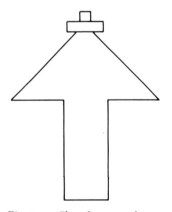

Fig. 2-21. Chamfer router bit.

27

Fig. 2-22. Straight router bit (1/4").

Fig. 2-23. Straight router bit (3/4").

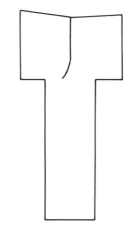

THE TURNING FUNCTION

The turning function is best accomplished with a wood lathe (Fig. 2-24). The lathe generally is used to make an entire project. Unlike many other large, floor-model tools, the lathe and the turning tools used with it confront the user with an exciting world of different projects. I will present some projects to be turned from pine. If you have never turned pine on your lathe, this is a good time to start. It is an excellent turning wood and can result in some very functional and decorative projects.

If you are looking for a single tool for getting involved in woodworking, give serious consideration to the lathe. Although an expensive tool, it is one of the most satisfying and enjoyable ways of working with wood. The projects presented will serve to introduce you to only a few of the many possibilities the lathe holds for turning wood.

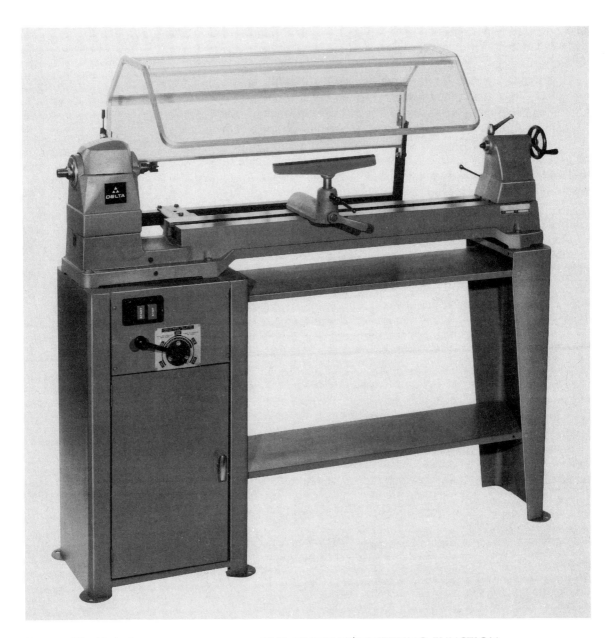

Fig. 2-24. Wood lathe (courtesy of Delta International Machinery Corp.).

THE CARVING/WHITTLING FUNCTION

Although carving and whittling are actually two different ways of working with wood, for our purposes they are combined. As with wood turning, this is an area that also is a totally self-contained function. I have included projects to introduce you to this extremely enjoyable, relaxing, and satisfying way of working with wood. While pine is not the best wood for carving some pieces, it is more than adequate for many others. Pine is also a good wood to use to develop some basic carving and whittling skills. As you will quickly discover as you begin exploring the world of carving tools, their numbers are almost overwhelming. In addition to the presented projects, you might want to examine some of the references presented in the Bibliography.

In addition to carving tools, there is a range of whittling knives available for the beginner. You might want to explore the literature of whittling. A number of books in the Bibliography discuss this fascinating method of working with wood. One device that I have found useful with some of my projects is a *scorp* (Fig. 2-25). This tool is extremely helpful for roughing out the bill of a wooden spoon. It also can be used for making small pine bowls. You will find that there are a great many different tools that can assist you in the whittling and carving function.

As you will discover quickly, one of the requirements of carving and whittling is being able to sharpen your knives and tools. Although I will briefly touch on this process in the projects, you would be well advised to do some additional reading. It is critical that your tools be extremely sharp. A dull tool or knife will not remove wood and it is very dangerous. Accidents happen in carving and whittling when your tools and knives are dull.

In recent years, increasing numbers of carvers have been using small electric tools for removing and shaping wood. For example, I frequently use either a commercial grinder and flex shaft tool or a Dremel tool. The small Dremel tool, along with drum sanders and various cutters, is extremely effective for both removing wood and shaping a project. Although they lack the romance and the satisfaction of using knives or tools, these tools are effective and very efficient. If you already have a small moto tool, you might want to consider buying a router attachment and some microrouter bits. With them, you can carve on the surfaces of projects.

I have found that carving and whittling are very much like wood turning. Once you get started, you don't want to quit. They are fascinating and thoroughly enjoyable ways of working wood and relaxing at the same time. I usually wear thick leather gloves when I carve or whittle. This procedure grows out of experience. I would recommend that you use some protective gear for your hands.

Although not a carving tool, one other device that is frequently used on carved pieces is a woodburning unit. Some carvers burn fine details into their carvings, particularly ducks. I frequently use a burning tool to enhance the lid of a box or the surface of some decorative project. You will be amazed

Fig. 2-25. Scorp.

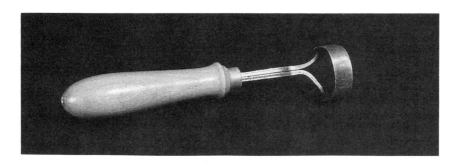

at how many projects look a bit sharper or more attractive if you do some decorative woodburning on them. In a number of projects, I suggest the use of one of these devices. If you are interested in purchasing a woodburning tool, review the various mail-order tool catalogs. I use a rather inexpensive one that came with a child's project kit. It is not the best in terms of continuous heat or detailed work, but it does the job for me. I hope you try some woodburning on one of your projects. I think you will thoroughly enjoy the process. By the way, do some practicing on scraps before you start on your finished project. Woodburning does take some getting used to, especially the first time you do it.

THE SANDING FUNCTION

Prior to assembling any of the parts of a project, you will need to sand the various surfaces. Abrasive papers and a number of tools to simplify this function are critical to a quality project. It is important to remember that you must remove the dust generated by sanding from all surfaces prior to gluing or applying any finishes.

Unlike many other functions in the woodworking process, sanding easily can be done by hand. You simply must remember to always sand *with* the grain of the wood. Most of the pine you buy for projects will need some sanding to clean and smooth the surfaces. Frequently there are stenciled grading marks on the board's surface. These marks are generally made with some type of ink and can be very difficult to remove. There are also any number of other marks and dirty spots on the surfaces that should be removed. Rough edges and sharp corners need to be lightly rolled with abrasive papers. Planing marks that give the board's surface a wavy appearance also need to be removed. You will find that finishing is much easier and the final project is more attractive when you have properly sanded a board.

Abrasive papers are available in a range of gifts. The numbering system that is used for abrasive papers tells you how coarse or fine the abrasive grit is. Some manufacturers simply refer to their abrasive papers as being fine, medium, or coarse. As a rule, the coarser the grit, the lower the number given the paper. For pine projects, I often start with 80-grit abrasive paper, followed by 100 grit, and finally 150 grit. You might want to use 220 grit on some of the projects, depending upon how you will finish it. With pine, these grits are generally adequate. This does not mean, however, that the surface is ideal. You very well might want to use even finer grits on your projects. A major part of the sanding process is deciding how much time you want to spend doing it.

Most abrasive papers are sold in 9-×-11-inch sheets. This is the most economical way to buy abrasive papers. You can tear the piece into any number of smaller pieces for a particular job. Most general-purpose abrasive papers have aluminum oxide as the grit. This type of abrasive is excellent for either using by hand or with a power sander.

A block of wood with abrasive paper wrapped around it is an effective procedure for sanding flat surfaces. A piece of carpet pad is an excellent backing for abrasive papers when you need to sand rounded surfaces. Of course, commercial sanding blocks made from cork or rubber are available if you want to buy one. I have found that making your own sanding blocks is both easy and inexpensive.

If you prefer power sanding, you can find a variety of available hand and floor-model power sanding tools. A range of hand and floor sanders use abrasive belts of various sizes. If you have a belt sander, especially a large 6-×-48-inch floor model, you are well prepared to sand the projects. This type of large belt sander has become a rather popular homeowner tool in recent years. If you are inclined toward production woodworking, you will find that the larger belt sander is almost mandatory. Most people, however, will have no need for such a large tool.

A palm or finishing sander is a type of power tool that you might want to consider purchasing. These small, electric finishing sanders are ideal for preparing the surfaces of projects. Most of them use a quarter sheet of standard 9-×-11-inch abrasive paper. In addition to local hardware and discount stores, shop the mail-order catalogs for these tools. There are usually some excellent buys available on either American or Japanese small power sanders. I always finish projects with these small palm sanders. They are effective, easy to use, and reasonably priced. It is hard to beat this combination in any tool.

Additional information and methods that are helpful in preparing projects for finishing are included in Chapter 4. You also might want to refer to some of the books in the Bibliography that deal with preparation of the surface for finishing. The final appearance of your project will be very much determined by how well you do the sanding function.

THE ASSEMBLING FUNCTION

While some projects require no assembly, others must be assembled using wood glue, nails, and sometimes screws. An array of products and devices is now available to help you assemble your projects with relative ease. You will find, however, that all projects do not need to be assembled in the same manner. How a piece is assembled is primarily determined by how the project will be used. With a large shelf, for example, you might want to use wood glue, nails, or screws. A small, decorative piece might require only glue for assembly. Items that will be subjected to constant use and stress need to be more securely assembled. Thus, as you approach the assembly of your projects, always review how you will use the piece.

Glue is the primary product used in assembling projects. A range of high-quality glues are available, but the standard yellow-colored (aliphatic resin) wood glue is best. There are any number of companies manufacturing high-quality aliphatic resin wood glue. When you are purchasing glue, be certain it is wood glue and not general-purpose white glue. White glue is adequate for gluing mirrors into frames or securing paper as backing on mirror frames; however, you should always use wood glue for assembling projects. Most local discount or hardware stores stock both types of glue. Also, they are always available through mail-order tool suppliers. If you are planning to do a number of projects, buy the large containers of glue. Do not let the glues, especially the yellow wood glue, freeze. Freezing will ruin it.

Although not mandatory, especially if you decide to use screws for assembling, clamps can be very useful. Whenever component parts of a project are glued together, they need to be clamped until the glue is dry. Clamping ensures a good bond between the pieces being assembled. A large variety of clamps are available to assist you in the clamping process. I have found the Jorgensen and Pony clamps to be very useful in my woodworking. The steel bar clamp is an excellent choice for general clamping work. Another excellent clamp for woodworking is the adjustable steel spindle handscrews. On larger projects, I usually use the adjustable Pony clamp fixtures that use black pipe. All of these clamps are available in a range of sizes, and they provide sufficient clamping versatility and holding power for pine projects. Clamps are not only effective for holding a joint together while the glue dries, they also allow you to clamp out a slight bow in a board when you are assembling.

Small C clamps also can be effective for clamping some of the smaller pine projects. These clamps are less expensive than bar clamps, but are also much smaller. You can, of course, buy them in a range of sizes. Before you buy any clamps, you might want to determine if you will need them for a particular project you want to make. Often screws and nails will eliminate the need for clamping.

Another device that can assist, not only in clamping but also for holding pieces that you are working on, is the wood vice. Although not a mandatory item for any of the projects, the wood vice can be extremely useful. To use it, you must secure it to a bench. You can use the vice to hold a piece of wood during the sawing process or while carving. Although various clamps can perform the same functions, a small wood vice can be very useful in the shop.

Although simple to use, nails can be rather complicated when it comes to knowing which type to use and when to use it. They can, however, be used with many of the projects in this book. Thus, some familiarity with them is important. Nails are highly standardized in terms of size, weight, length, type of head, and appropriate use. In addition to commonly used nails, you will discover that there are many specialty nails, such as screw nails or corrugated nails. For the projects, you need to be familiar primarily with the finishing nail.

The size of nails is measured in a *penny* system abbreviated *d*. This system was originally based on the number of a particular size nail that could be bought for a penny. Today, the smaller the number, the smaller the nail. For example, a 2d nail is 1 inch long, while a 60 d nail is 6 inches long. Most hardware stores have charts depicting the various sizes and types of nails using the penny system.

The finishing nail is used primarily for indoor work, furniture making, and crafts. The head of the nail is not much wider than the body, and thus is easily driven under the board's surface. Driving the head under the surface is done using a nail set. Nail sets come with different diameters at their points for use on different sizes of nail heads. You can fill the nail hole with wood putty and thus remove any holes in the surface. In length, finishing nails are 3d (1¼ inches), 4d (1½ inches), 6d (2 inches), 8d (2½ inches), and 10d (3 inches). For most projects requiring finishing nails, 3d or 4d nails are usually adequate.

On occasion, you might want to use small brads and escutcheon pins. These and a range of other naillike devices are readily available and can serve important functions in the crafting process. A small tack hammer is useful for driving in finishing nails, wire brads, and small pins. It also helps prevent you from smashing your fingers with one of the larger hammers. You might want to examine the variety of these devices in your local hardware store. It is always helpful to have some idea of what is available.

For some projects, you might prefer using wood screws instead of finishing nails. For example, you can easily assemble shelves using wood screws. When using screws, I drill a ⅜- or ½-inch-diameter hole in the board's surface to accommodate the head of the screw. After the screws are in place, I glue a wood plug of the appropriate diameter into the screw hole. I then sand the plug flush with the surface. This process hides the screws, and also gives the piece the appearance of a plug-assembled project.

Screws are highly standardized and available in a range of styles and differing head configurations. Their primary advantage over nails is their holding power. They do, however, require considerably more time and effort to use than do nails. As a rule, I use flathead wood screws when a project requires this type of assembly. I also tend to purchase the least expensive screws. As a guide, screws should penetrate the board being secured by at least one-half of their length. Obviously, the more penetration, the better the holding power.

You might want to explore the range of available wood screws at a local hardware store. Flathead, Phillips wood screws are generally the easiest to drive into the wood. You also might want to examine some of the new square, recess screws. A good technique to ease the penetration of screws into wood is to rub a little soap on the threads. Be careful not to buy screws with a diameter that is too large for the thickness of the wood. It is very easy to crack a board when you are securing it with a screw that is too large.

If you are interested in using pneumatic tools and have an air compressor, you might want to consider a power nailer or stapler. Although these tools are for those who plan to make projects in quantity, they are excellent for assembling. I have used both a power nailer and stapler for many years. They greatly speedup the assembly process and secure the various parts with nails or staples coated with a substance to provide additional holding power. The nails and staples come in strips and are quickly inserted into tools. Both are available in a range of lengths.

Although the foregoing discussion briefly presents the major functions and some of the tools used in the crafting process, it does not include the various issues and procedures for finishing the projects. Chapter 4 addresses the finishing function and also the various procedures and devices for hanging completed projects. More specific functions in the project-making process are discussed in detail in individual projects. Additionally, I will discuss a number of minor, yet critical, tools that are used with various projects.

CRAFTING SUPPLIES

Although you can craft most of the projects totally from lumber that you purchase at the local dealer, some projects require commercially made component parts. You might prefer to make some of these parts yourself. Following are commercial products, as well as suggestions to assist you in making these components.

In recent years, there has emerged a range of manufacturers and mail-order suppliers who specialize in crafting supplies. The range of these products, their quality, availability, and price make them ideal for use with your pine projects. Items or components that were previously available only to commercial wood-product manufacturers, now are available to the general public. There are speciality items available for almost any project you might want to undertake. Any number of these items will be useful with the various projects presented in the next chapter.

One type of item that you will definitely want to consider purchasing is Shaker pegs (Fig. 2-26). These pegs are critical to a number of the pine projects that you will be crafting. The pegs, designed by the Early American Shaker community, are marvels of function and beauty. As you will discover in a number of the projects, Shaker pegs can be used for hanging bathrobes, cups, coats, or anything else that needs a place. Although you can make a similar functional peg from a standard dowel, the commercially available Shaker pegs make your crafting easier and, I believe, much more fun. The price of the commercial pegs makes them affordable for the hobbyist woodworker. You will find a number of mail-order suppliers of Shaker pegs and other components listed in the Appendix. Incidentally, Shaker pegs are also available in a range of sizes. When they are required for a particular project, I will indicate the necessary size.

Other wood component parts that you might want to consider buying are candle cups (Fig. 2-27). These and the brass rings that you can use with them are readily available from a number of mail-order suppliers. Although

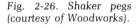
Fig. 2-26. Shaker pegs (courtesy of Woodworks).

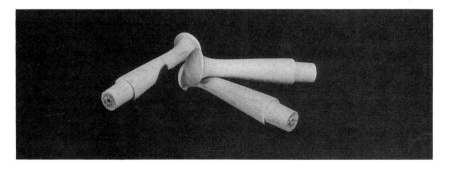

you can drill holes of an appropriate size to accommodate the base of a candle, these commercial cups greatly enhance your projects.

Gallery rail spindles, which can be used on plate shelves, are another delightful commercial item (Fig. 2-28). These small spindles are available in a range of sizes and greatly enhance a railing around the top surface of a shelf. Although you can use pieces of dowel, the commercial spindles present a more formal appearance to a finished shelf.

Screwhole plugs and buttons are another commercial item that you might want to consider. Although you can cut plugs with standard plug cutters on a drill press, the commercial ones are easier to use and more uniform in size. The small wood buttons provide an attractive touch to a number of projects.

There are many other commercially available components that you might want to use with your projects, but the ones listed here can be used with the presented projects. You will find, as you explore the various mail-order catalogs, that the variety of component parts available is a veritable bonanza for the home crafter.

For many years I have ordered most of my crafting supplies and tools from mail-order suppliers. In general, the companies have been reliable and guarantee their products and service. An added feature of mail-order shopping

Fig. 2-27. Candle cups and brass rings (courtesy of Woodworks).

Fig. 2-28. Gallery rails (courtesy of Woodworks).

is the availability of toll-free telephone numbers. Most companies are also willing to discuss their products via toll-free numbers. To facilitate your shopping, almost all accept national credit cards.

As you will find in the Appendix, most mail-order companies have catalogs and other descriptive literature of their products. Usually there is a charge for the catalog, but the amount is often deducted from the first order you place. Given the cost of printing and postage, it is not unreasonable for suppliers to charge for their catalogs. I also have found that catalogs from many of these companies can be an effective way to learn about woodworking. Another significant aspect of mail-order catalogs is the fantasy value they can provide. They represent the ultimate wish book for anyone who is faintly interested in woodworking.

The Appendix includes a sampling of mail-order suppliers of both crafting products and tools. It also provides a listing of various woodworking magazines.

Chapter 3

Projects from Pine

Unlike other crafting books that provide very detailed plans and precise dimensions for wood projects, this book will approach the tasks somewhat differently. In part, small pine projects do not require this type of crafting detail. Also, projects that are country in theme probably look better if they are somewhat rough dimensionally and in design. They certainly are much easier to make. For each project, a photograph of the assembled piece is presented to assist you. In some instances, the pictured project will be stained and finished. Other project pictures will present items that are unfinished. The various projects that are designed for the tole painter are unfinished and unpainted. Although I will make narrative suggestions regarding possible use of the projects, I do not include the specifics on painting. Throughout this chapter, when necessary or deemed helpful, I will present drawings of component parts or assemblies, with some dimensions. On occasion, there are also drawings of alternative designs.

I will suggest general materials and supplies necessary for making a particular project. I also will give a number of specific tasks that are deemed critical for a project, along with suggestions for tools and their usage. Additionally, I will provide a few tips and an occasional shortcut. However, an overriding theme of my approach to making small pine projects is to encourage you to use your own resources and creativity. Much of the pleasure in woodworking is to solve the problems of your projects and have the opportunity to use your own imagination in designing and crafting your work.

My approach not only makes the entire process more satisfying, but also will be more practical: you can make things in the size and way that you want and need. For example, some of the projects are 18-, and 24-inch-long shelves. Although these are functional dimensions for a shelf, they might not meet your specific need. Thus, you are encouraged to redesign them to dimensions that you want. Similarly, a general leg design is provided for each shelf, along with some alternatives. If their shape or dimensions do not appeal to you, redesign them. You are making projects for your house, and your needs should determine the dimensional and design outcome of the project.

This approach to making projects will, in part, eliminate the constant worry of doing something wrong—of making a mistake. Failures are usually the result of trying to exactly duplicate something that another person has designed. Frequently, in trying to follow all the intricate details of a project, you become frustrated, fail to do things according to directions, and generally have a miserable time. I prefer that you concentrate on and enjoy the wood and the process of woodworking. Make your projects, using the general designs and dimensions as ideas, in the way that you want them to look. This approach in making projects greatly reduces the inappropriate fears of making a mistake and, frankly, makes for better final pieces.

One final note before you begin the actual crafting process. As you will note, each project is numbered and has a brief descriptive heading. To eliminate duplication of some detailed procedures, I will state them once and provide a reference to them when required by a later project. For example, I will give the procedures for using a table-mounted router to round over the edges of a board but once. Later projects that require the same procedure will have only a reference to the earlier discussion. You might want to refer back to it to brush up on the various procedures. Hopefully, after you have done the procedure once, you will not need to refer to earlier discussions. Enjoy yourself.

PROJECT 1: STANDARD SHELF

I have not indicated any specific function for the Standard Shelf (Fig. 3-1), only the width and thickness of the shelf top. Its length is your decision, based

Fig. 3-1. Standard Shelf.

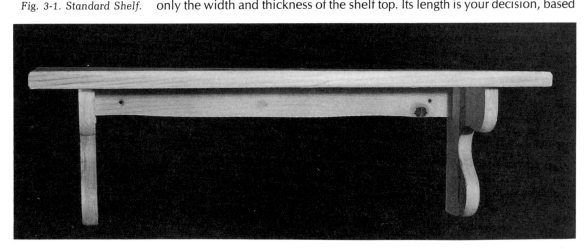

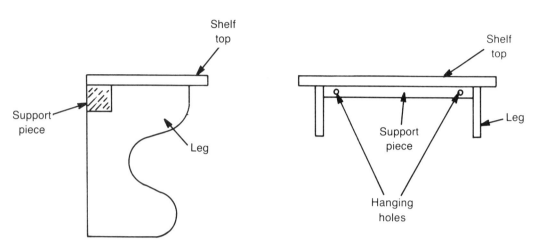

Side view   Front view

Shelf
top

Support
piece

Leg

Shelf
top

Leg

Support
piece

Hanging
holes

on where you need and want a shelf and what its purpose will be. Measure the area where you plan to hang the shelf and then build it to the exact length needed. Figure 3-2 presents the front and side views of a general shelf design. These drawings and terms will serve as reference points for making shelves.

As a rule, I make and use patterns in my woodworking whether I am building a shelf or some other project (Fig. 3-3). For a shelf of this design,

Fig. 3-2. Standard Shelf: front and side views.

Fig. 3-3. Metal project patterns.

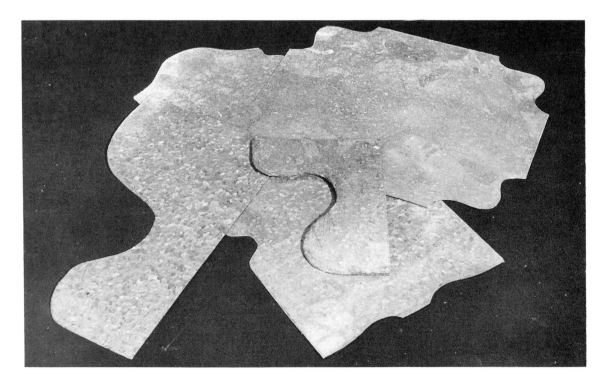

you only need one pattern, for making the legs. Patterns are rather fun to make, and they are critical to the designing and crafting process. They ensure uniformity of size and design, and they also make sawing the needed piece substantially easier. Heavy construction paper is excellent material for making initial patterns. This type of paper is sufficiently durable, but it is also easy to cut with a pair of scissors. Patterns using this type of paper allow you to explore ideas and possible designs with relative ease and without wasting wood. They enable you to get some perspective of size and appearance before you begin the actual crafting process. Always make patterns to the actual desired size of the part or design and then trace the pattern onto the wood's surface for cutting. In the cutting function, you simply follow the traced pattern lines. The only other consideration in using patterns is to trace them with the grain of the wood, rather than across the grain. Figure 3-4 presents a drawing of a leg pattern that I frequently use on standard shelves. It is not drawn to its actual size, but the dimensions generally used are provided.

I have found this pattern to be a reasonably useful design for the legs of a 1-×-8-inch Standard Shelf. Its size seems in good proportion to the top whether that is 12 or 36 inches long. If you want to use this design or modify it according to your own tastes, make and cut a pattern to the appropriate dimensions. Incidentally, when you are making a pattern, use the side and top edges of the pattern paper for the top and back of the shelf legs. In this

Fig. 3-4. Leg pattern.

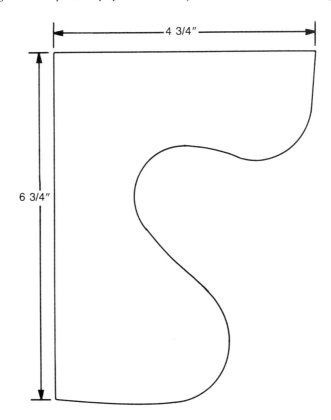

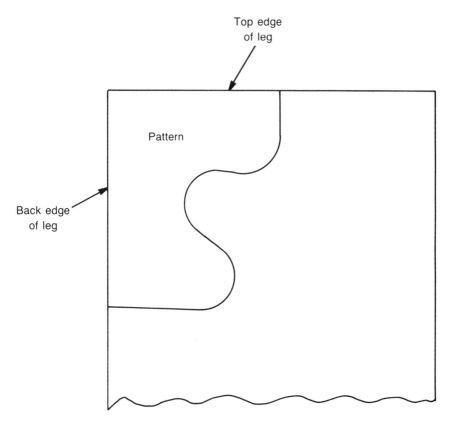

Top edge
of leg

Pattern

Back edge
of leg

way, you will have good, straight edges on your pattern (Fig. 3-5). You can draw the curved, front portion of the shelf leg pattern freehand or use anything handy that is round. You can use a coffee or paint can, cup, saucer, glass, or some other object for making a partial or complete circle. Use your imagination when you are making patterns, especially when you need to make a curve.

Fig. 3-5. Shelf leg on construction paper.

Figure 3-6 presents a few options for leg designs that you also can use with a standard shelf. To some extent, these optional designs are easier to pattern and saw, especially if you lack power tools. You might want to spend some time designing a totally different leg configuration. As suggested, much of the fun in crafting is developing your own unique designs. Shelf legs afford you an excellent opportunity to explore your own design ideas.

Let's assume that you have decided to make your 1-×-8-inch Standard Shelf 24 inches long. As you plan your material needs, you will need a minimum, allowing for waste, of at least 4 feet of pine. Although you can get by with less, usually some portions of No. 3 Common boards are not usable. When you are planning your material needs, always buy a bit more than the project actually requires. A number of later projects present a few ways to maximize any scraps. If you decide to put a support piece on the back of your shelf, you will need some additional material. Refer to Fig. 3-2 to see how the support piece relates to the top and legs of the shelf design.

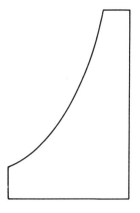

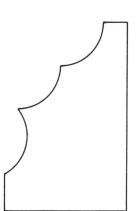

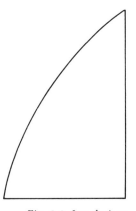

Fig. 3-6. Leg designs.

The support piece on a shelf generally provides the means for hanging the shelf on the wall. It also makes the shelf top and legs sturdier because it ties them together. Another purpose of the support piece is to make the entire shelf more attractive. Generally, the support piece will be from 4 to 6 inches shorter than the shelf top. This length allows for a 2- or 3-inch overlap between the edge of the shelf top and the legs, on both sides. As a rule of thumb, the longer the shelf, the more the shelf top should overlap the legs. Figure 3-7 depicts the support piece in relation to the shelf top and its overlap.

Note that, in Fig. 3-7, the support piece is *flush*, or even, with the outside edge of the legs. Generally, I use standard 1-inch-thick material and make the support piece 1¼ inches wide. These dimensions, especially on a shelf that will carry considerable weight, are usually adequate. On smaller shelves or those that will support only a minimum of weight, I rip the support piece to an approximate thickness of ½ inch. Hopefully, you will have some scrap lumber from which you can cut the support pieces, and you will not need to cut into new material.

[1] As stated, to make a 1-×-8-×-24-inch Standard Shelf, you will need at least 4 feet of pine. If you have decided on a different length for your shelf, purchase your material in relation to this length. You also need wood for the support piece. A piece of 1 × 4 that is 2 feet in length is adequate for a 24-inch-long shelf. You should have sufficient material leftover for a number of support pieces for other shelves you might want to make.

[2] Because boards seldom have clean, square ends, it is always a good practice to cut off an inch or so from one end. Using a try square, make a straight cutting line on the board's surface and saw off the end piece. Whether you use a hand saw, power saber saw, or floor-model power saw, be certain to follow the marked line so you have a straight, square end.

[3] Using either a tape or some other measuring device and starting from the squared end of the board, measure and mark a 24-inch-long section. This piece will be the top of the shelf. If you are making a shelf of a different length, lay out the top piece to the desired dimension. If you are using a hand or saber saw, again make a straight cutting line using a try square. Cut the board to length.

It is a good practice to wear either a protective face shield or safety glasses when you are woodworking, especially when you are using tools. You also might want to wear some type of dust mask. You also should wear ear plugs, especially when you are using power tools. Be certain you are totally familiar with the tools you are planning to use, especially power tools.

[4] Your leg pattern should be finished and ready to use. If not, decide on the design and dimensions you want and make the pattern to the actual size of the leg. Place the pattern on the wood, making sure the top edge is flush with a squared end of the board and the back edge is flush with the edge of the board. This procedure will give you two straight edges and will eliminate the need to make two cuts. Reverse the pattern and trace the second leg onto the board's surface. You should trace both legs with the grain

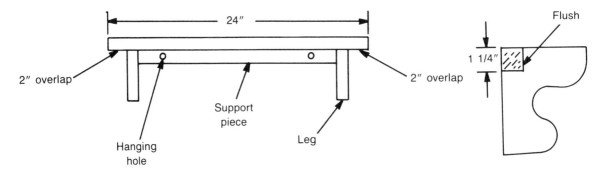

2" overlap

24"

Hanging
hole

Support
piece

Leg

2" overlap

Flush

1 1/4"

Fig. 3-7. Shelf with support piece.

of the wood. When pieces are traced with the grain, they are stronger and less likely to split. They are also more attractive than pieces traced across the grain (Fig. 3-8).

After you have traced the two legs on the board, cut them out. A power saber saw with a fine-toothed blade will do an excellent job on cutting both the straight edge and the curves. You will need to support or clamp the board to a solid surface while you are cutting out the legs. Hopefully, you will have a pair of saw horses, an old table, or some other way to support the board during cutting. In any event, think safety when you are using a power tool.

Fig. 3-8. Leg tracing process.

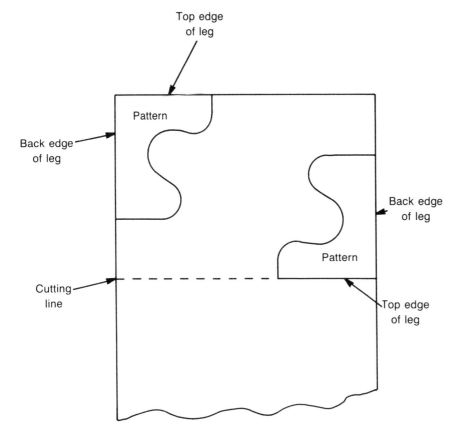

Top edge
of leg

Pattern

Back edge
of leg

Back edge
of leg

Pattern

Cutting
line

Top edge
of leg

44

[5] The next component you need to measure and cut is the shelf support piece. Refer to Fig. 3-7 for the placement of the support piece. As indicated earlier, the length of the support piece will determine how much of an overlap will be on both edges of the top shelf. With a 24-inch-long shelf top, I generally have a 2-inch overlap on each side. Thus, the support piece should be 20 inches long. If you are making a shelf of a different length, modify the length of the support piece accordingly.

Rather than waste 1-×-8 material, I generally cut the support pieces from 1-×-4 stock. To be effective, the piece should be at least 1¼ inches wide and the thickness of the stock. In laying out and measuring the support piece, use one edge of the board as one edge of the support piece. It is usually a good, straight edge and will save you some time and cutting. After you have cut the support piece to length and width, drill two holes through it using a countersink drill bit or similar device. The holes should be about 3 inches from each end of the support piece. These holes are for screws, nails, or whatever else you want to use to hang the shelf. Figure 3-9 presents the layout of the support piece on the board and also the finished component.

[6] In order to secure the two legs to the support piece, you must trace and cut an area from the back of the legs. Place the end of the support piece against the side surface of a leg, flush with the top and back edge. Trace an outline of the support end onto the leg's surface. Follow this procedure for the other leg, as well. Figure 3-10 shows how the leg will appear after this

Fig. 3-9. Support piece.

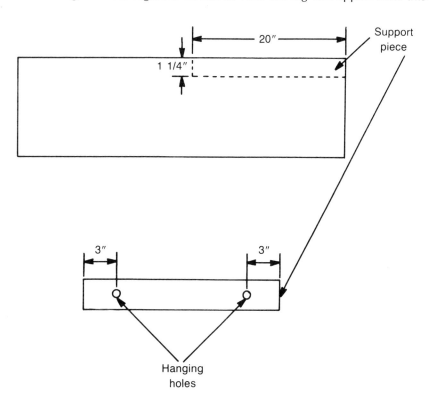

45

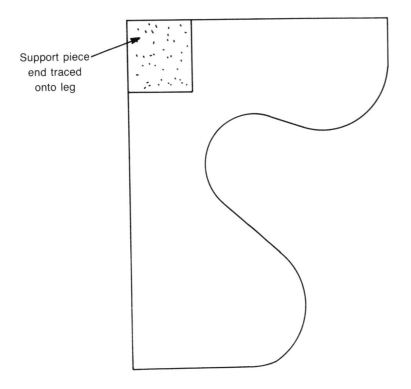

Support piece
end traced
onto leg

Fig. 3-10. Leg with support
piece traced on its side.

tracing procedure. It also indicates the area of the leg that must be cut out to hold the support piece in place.

Using a saber saw or a handsaw, carefully cut out the traced area from both legs. Cut on the penciled lines so that you will have a good fit when you assemble the support piece and leg. Be certain to support the leg on a solid surface during the cutting process.

[7] Before you assemble the shelf, you should rout and sand the various edges of all the parts, except the support piece. If you do not have a table-mounted router, you can round over the edges with 100-grit abrasive paper.

A table-mounted router, as discussed in Chapter 2, is the preferable way to prepare the edges of the various parts of the shelf. On this type of shelf, I usually round the edges. For this step, you will need either a ⅜- or ½-inch round-over or quarter-round router bit. Before you proceed with the routing function, review the various safety and user information that accompanies this tool. The router is a very unforgiving tool, and one that you must use very carefully. Always wear both ear and eye protectors when you are using this tool.

Set the router bit to the desired depth of cut. I usually run a test board over the bit to determine if the cut is set properly. A piece of scrap works fine for this procedure. Do not set the depth of cut too deep. Too radical a cut not only spoils the appearance of the piece, but is also dangerous. As a rule, I only round over the edges enough to remove the sharpness and give them a slightly rolled appearance. There is no need to actually make the edges round. I am inclined to think that many users remove too much wood with the router (see Fig. 3-11).

Do not rout the edges of the support piece. You want to leave the sharp edges of the support piece so that they will fit neatly into the cutout areas of the legs. Rout the shelf top on all edges except the bottom edge that will rest on the support piece. You want to have sharp edges where the shelf top and support piece come together. Rout only the face edges of the legs and a portion of the back edges. Do not rout the top edges of the legs. Here, again, you want sharp edges where the legs will be attached to the bottom surface of the shelf top. On the back edges of the legs, I stop routing about ¼ inch below the support-piece cutouts so there are sharp edges for the attachment of the legs and support piece. Figure 3-12 shows the areas on the legs that should be routed.

[8] After you have completed the routing function and before you assemble the project, sand the various edges and surfaces. It is much easier to prepare all surfaces for the finishing process before you assemble the shelf. Before you begin routing or sanding, decide which side of the shelf piece will be the top. You should always put the best board's surface facing down. Remember, you will not see the top of the shelf after it is hung and covered with items. Thus, you want the best side facing down. I am always amazed at how many people, when buying a shelf, make a selection based on how attractive the top of the shelf appears. When you are selecting a shelf, always examine the bottom surface of the top, the support piece, and the legs. These are the things that will be seen when the shelf is in place. It is good to remember this fact when you are making and finishing your shelves.

Using a selection of abrasive papers—80, 100, and 150 grit—begin the process of sanding the surfaces of the various components. This is the time that a small, electric finishing sander is ideal. If you do not have one, fold the abrasive paper in two pieces or wrap it over a small block of wood or piece of carpet for sanding. Always sand with the grain, beginning with the

Fig. 3-11. Routing the shelf top on a table-mounted router.

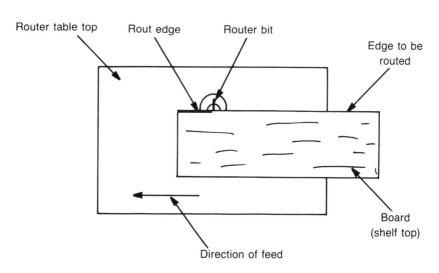

Router table top · Rout edge · Router bit

Edge to be routed

Board (shelf top)

Direction of feed

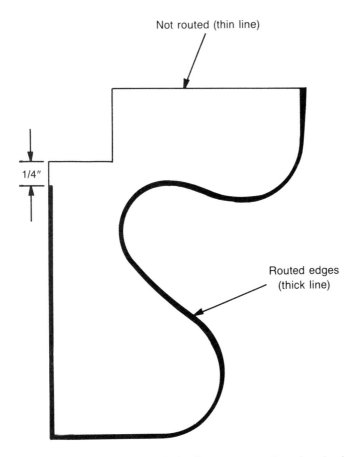

Not routed (thin line)

1/4"

Routed edges
(thick line)

coarsest grit abrasive on up through the finest. Remember that the lower the abrasive grit number, the coarser the paper. Thus, 80 grit is considered coarse, while 150 grit is considered fine.

Sand the routed edges, but do not sand the nonrouted edges of the various parts. You want to leave sharp and straight edges for assembly. Wear a dust mask when sanding.

After you have finished sanding, wipe all surfaces with a rag. You want to remove any dust from areas that will be glued because dust prevents glue from doing its job. If you have an air compressor, use it for blowing away the accumulation of sawdust. A slightly dampened rag is also a good method for removing sawdust from the surfaces. Too much water on the rag, however, will stain the wood.

[9] The first assembling task is to join the two legs and the support piece. Using yellow wood glue, spread a bead on the two cut edges of a leg where the support piece will fit. Start two finishing nails in each end of the support piece, one above the other. Place the nails so that they will penetrate into the center portion of the leg. The two countersunk drill holes that you made in the face of the support piece should be facing out toward the front of the shelf. With the nails started and the glue spread, set the support piece in the

Fig. 3-12. Areas to be routed.

leg cutout. Place the front edge of the leg against a hard surface and drive in the two nails. Be certain the edge of the support piece and the outer surface of the leg are flush before nailing. Also, be certain the leg is straight in relation to the support piece. You do not want to have a crooked leg under the shelf top. Figure 3-13 depicts the placement and assembly of a leg and the support piece.

Using a damp cloth, wipe off any excess glue that might squeeze out during this assembling procedure. The glue stains the wood, so you want to remove any excess from the surfaces. Also, wood stain does not cover glue that remains on the surface. It cannot penetrate into the wood through the glue. Remember, more glue is not better.

Repeat this assembly process with the other leg. If you have an air-powered nailer, this assembly procedure is very quick and easy. It is one of the many tasks that a pneumatic nailer does well.

Incidentally, you can use screws in place of finishing nails to secure the support piece to the legs, if you desire. Drill pilot holes through the support piece to receive the screws and then secure them to the legs. Screws will make for a much stronger shelf. When you are using screws, you also want to use wood glue.

[10] Before you assemble the legs and support assembly to the shelf top, be certain that the top edges of the legs and the support piece are flush. If they are not, sand them flush. You want the surfaces of the legs and support piece to make good contact with the bottom of the shelf piece. It not only looks better, but makes for a more secure shelf.

Fig. 3-13. Support piece and leg assembly process.

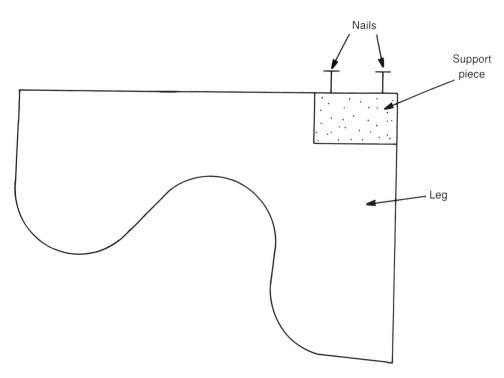

Nails

Support
piece

Leg

[11] Place the shelf piece, top face down, on a clean surface. Remember, you have sanded all the pieces so you do not want to get them dirty or scratched. Set the leg and support assembly, as it will be assembled, on the shelf piece. Mark the exact location of the leg assembly on the bottom surface of the shelf piece. The shelf top must overlap the same distance from each leg. Place the assembly flush with the unrouted bottom edge of the shelf piece. Using the dimensions of our sample shelf, the outer surface of the legs should be 2 inches from the edges of the shelf piece. You will need a ruler to make these measurements. When one end of the assembly is exactly 2 inches from the edge, the other should be also. Place small pencil marks on the surface of the shelf piece where each leg should be secured. Also, make marks on the back edge of the shelf piece at the same locations. You will use these marks for alignment when you secure the leg assembly and the shelf top together. Figure 3-14 depicts these procedures.

To assist you in nailing the shelf top to the leg assembly, you might want to mark points on the top surface of the shelf where the nails should be placed. Use the alignment marks on the back edge of the shelf piece as guides. You might want to use a try square for this marking procedure. Be certain to place the nail marks ⅜ inch in from the alignment marks. Remember, the alignment marks are at the outer edge of the legs. By moving the nails in from these marks by ⅜ inch, you will place them directly over the center of the legs. Also, remember that the legs do not extend the entire width of the shelf top. I generally drive two finishing nails into each leg and three into the support piece. Figure 3-15 depicts the layout for nailing the shelf top to the leg assembly.

[12] Spread a bead of glue on the top surfaces of both legs and on the total length of the support piece. Smear the glue around with your finger. You will want to use extra glue on the legs because their surfaces are cross-grain. A cross-grain surface tends to absorb the glue more quickly, so you must use extra. Do not use too much glue on any of the surfaces, since it will squeeze out when you assemble the components. With the shelf top laying

Fig. 3-14. Aligning the leg assembly and shelf top.

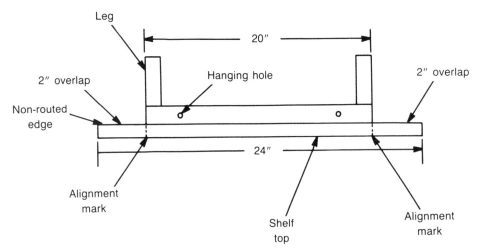

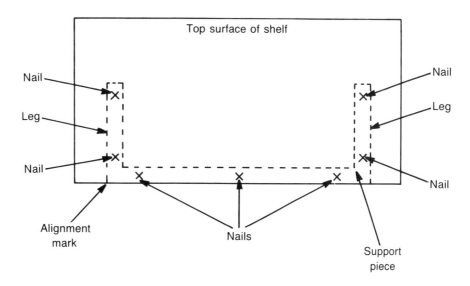

Top view

Top surface of shelf

Nail

Leg

Nail

Nail

Leg

Nail

Alignment mark

Nails

Support piece

Top view

Fig. 3-15. Nailing the leg assembly to the shelf top.

on a flat surface, bottom surface up, place the glued leg assembly between the alignment marks. Place it carefully so you do not smear glue around on the shelf surface. Be certain the back edge of the support piece is flush with the back edge of the shelf top. Press the assembly down and allow the glue to begin to dry.

After the glue begins to set up, turn over the entire assembly carefully and stand it on the two legs. Although this procedure is somewhat awkward, it can be done. Drive the first finishing nail in at the center of the support piece. Be sure to drive the nail from the top surface of the shelf into the center of the support piece. You can drive the nail while the glued assembly rests against one hand. Drive the second nail into the end area of the support piece.

When these two nails are in place, the assembly will hold together and you can drive the remaining nails into the legs and the support piece. Check to see that the top edges of the legs are flush against the bottom surface of the shelf piece. If not, lightly tap them into place. If you are having problems nailing the shelf together, have someone hold the glued assembly while you drive in the nails. You also can use bar clamps to secure the leg assembly and shelf top while you are nailing them.

[13] After the nails are all in place, use a nail punch to drive their heads under the board's surface. If you are interested in production woodworking, these kinds of jobs are well suited for a pneumatic nailer. With an air-powered nailer, these types of assembling tasks can be done in a matter of seconds. The nailers also countersink the nails as they are driven into the boards.

As suggested earlier, you can use the foregoing procedures to make a Standard Shelf of any length and width. You might want to make a shelf from 10- or even 12-inch-wide stock. The tasks would be the same.

PROJECT 2: SHAKER PEG SHELF

One of my favorite shelf designs is what I call a Shaker Peg Shelf (Fig. 3-16). I use this description because the project uses traditional pegs, designed by the Shakers. These pegs reflect the genius of these Early American woodworkers. Their design allows the user to hang almost anything on them.

This shelf design is usually made from 8-inch-wide stock. While the shelf can be used for storage or display, the pegs can be used for coats, cups, bathrobes, towels, children's items, and almost anything else you might want to hang on them. The Shakers hung chairs on the pegs while cleaning the floors. I have made this shelf in various lengths up to 6 feet. It is an excellent design to use over the partial or entire length of a wall in any room or hallway. Be sure to increase the number of Shaker pegs as you increase the length. Place the pegs in relation to whatever you will hang on them. If desired, you also can rout a groove in the top surface of the shelf to allow plates to be displayed. Project 3 presents the procedures for making this groove.

As with other projects, you should determine the exact length of the shelf needed. Although this shelf can be made somewhat smaller than 24 inches in length, a smaller design tends to cluster the pegs too closely together. For our purposes, I will use a shelf that is 24 inches long. The tasks and procedures for making the shelf are essentially the same, regardless of length. For a number of tasks, I will refer you back to the discussions in Project 1. If you already have made the Standard Shelf, hopefully you will remember how to do some of the procedures and will not need to refer to the earlier discussion.

[1] To make the Shaker Shelf to the dimensions suggested, 1 × 8 × 24 inches, you will need at least 4 feet of 1-×-8 pine. You also will need

Fig. 3-16. Shaker peg shelf.

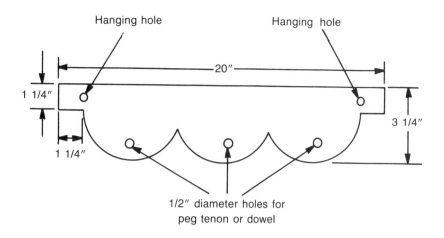

Hanging hole   Hanging hole

20"

1 1/4"

3 1/4"

1 1/4"

1/2" diameter holes for
peg tenon or dowel

Fig. 3-17. Shaker peg shelf's support piece.

least 2 feet of 1-×-4 stock for the support piece. Although you can get by with less 1-×-8 material, you need to allow for waste and some unusable portions of the board. When you select your pine for the shelf, be sure the board will provide an acceptable piece for the shelf top. Examine the board carefully and select a piece that is straight and acceptable for a shelf top.

[2] With your material at hand, square one end of the board using a try square or similar device. Cut the board end square. Measure and cut the shelf top piece to a length of 24 inches.

[3] The two legs for the Shaker Shelf are the same as those used for the Standard Shelf in Project 1. Both the design and the dimensions are the same. This is a good example of how useful patterns can be. Once you have a design that you are satisfied with, you can use it for any number of different projects.

Prepare a pattern or use the old one. Trace and cut the legs. You might want to refer to the extensive discussion and drawings of these procedures presented in Project 1.

[4] The support piece for the Shaker Shelf not only ties the legs together and supports the shelf when hung, it also holds the Shaker pegs. This piece is best made from 1-×-4 stock. Its width minimizes material waste when 4-inch-wide stock is used. If you do not have 1-×-4 material, you can easily cut the support piece from wider stock. It is simply a bit wasteful of wood. Figure 3-17 presents the support piece and its various dimensions for the 24-inch-long sample shelf.

As discussed in Project 1, the support piece is of a length that allows the shelf top to overlap the legs. With a 24-inch-long shelf top, I generally plan for a 2-inch overlap on both sides. As Fig. 3-17 indicates, the support piece therefore should be 20 inches long. On shelves with long tops, I increase the size of the overlap to make the shelf look balanced. For example, with a shelf top that is 36 inches long, I allow a 3-inch overlap at both ends.

The support piece for the Shaker Shelf should be at least 3¼ inches wide. This width enhances the appearance of the shelf, and also provides sufficient wood for the pegs to be secured into drilled holes.

To prepare the support piece, you either can make a pattern by taping pieces of construction paper together, or you can make the design freehand on the wood's surface. My own pattern for the support piece is made from wood. It is an actual support piece, laid out freehand, that I keep as a pattern. In addition to the details of the support piece, it also has the peg holes drilled in the proper locations. Incidentally, I always place the pegs exactly 5½ inches apart on a 24-inch-long shelf. Depending upon what you plan to hang on the pegs, this distance can be increased or decreased. I have found that 5½ inches provides sufficient distance between pegs for hanging most items.

A good procedure for making uniform curves for the support piece is to use a 2-pound coffee can or its plastic lid. These types of devices, in varying diameters, are excellent for making scrollwork designs on projects. You do need to measure so that the scrolls are of equal length, however.

As you pattern the support piece, make the ends about 1¼ inches wide and at least 1¼ inches long. These end sections will fit in cutout areas in the back of the legs. Refer to Fig. 3-17 to get a better idea of how the support piece should look when cut. A saber saw with a fine-toothed blade is an excellent tool to use to cut out the patterned support piece. It is especially effective in cutting the various scrolls. If you have a large floor-model scroll saw or jigsaw, the cutting procedures will go that much faster. You also can cut the piece using a band saw with a ⅛-inch-wide blade. Cut the support piece using the tool of your choice.

[5] Whether you plan to use commercial Shaker pegs or ½-inch-diameter dowels, the three holes in the support piece must be ½ inch in diameter. Shaker pegs have a standardized ½-inch-diameter tapered tenon. Measure and mark the placement of the peg holes on the support piece. As stated, I usually place the pegs 5½ inches apart. You should allow at least 1 inch from the bottom edge of the support piece to the peg holes. This distance is necessary for appearance but, more importantly, for strength. If you place a peg too close to the edge, it will break out when you hang something heavy on it. It also will break out when you drive the tapered tenon of the Shaker peg into the drilled hole. Be certain the peg holes are lined up with one another. Using your drill and an appropriate ½-inch-diameter bit, make the peg holes all the way through the support piece. I usually use a ½-inch brad-point or power bit to drill the holes.

For hanging the shelf, you also should drill a countersunk hole on each end of the support piece. Refer to Fig. 3-17 for the placement of these holes. Although you might decide later to use some other device to hang the shelf with, it is a good practice to drill hanging holes while you have the chance.

[6] Before you can do any assembly or sanding of surfaces, all edges need to be routed. If you do not have a table-mounted router, you can roll over the edges using abrasive paper. This rolling over process enchances the appearance of the shelf, and it also eliminates splinter-producing sharp edges. Refer to the discussion in Project 1 for procedures on routing the shelf top and legs. In this design, you also must rout the scroll edges of the support piece. Do not rout the top edge of the support piece or the two ends that

will be secured to the legs. Also, do not overrout any of the pieces. Only a very slight roll is needed on the various edges. If you are using only hand tools, a small block plane is effective in rolling the sharp edges of the shelf top.

[7] Before you place the Shaker pegs or any other assembly work, you should sand all surfaces and some edges. It is much easier to bring all the parts to finishing readiness before they are assembled. Using a range of abrasive grits, sand all the surfaces and the edges that you have routed. Do not roll over the sharp edges of those parts that will be joined to other parts. You also should roll the corners of the shelf top. Remember to always sand with the grain of the wood. After sanding is completed, wipe off the dust. Be certain you blow out the dust that has gathered in the drilled peg holes.

[8] If you plan to use commercial pegs, spread wood glue on the tenons and drive them into the three holes in the support piece. Do not use too much glue, or it will squeeze out on the support piece surface when you drive the pegs into their holes. For added strength, I spread some glue on the end of the tenons and walls of the back side of the support piece.

For driving the pegs into their holes, I often use a wooden mallet. You also can use a standard hammer with a small block of wood between the hammer and the peg's surface to prevent damage to the peg's surface while you are driving it into its hole.

As suggested, you can use ½-inch-diameter dowels in place of the commercial Shaker pegs. To make your pegs from dowels, cut three pieces of dowel 3½ inches long. Cut a notch or groove in each dowel piece about ½ inch from one end. A utility knife is an effective tool to use for making the cut (Fig. 3-18). The purpose of the notch is to prevent cups, coats, or whatever else you might hang on the dowel from sliding off the end. Figure 3-19 shows how the dowel piece should appear with its notch.

Spread glue on the ends of the dowels and drive them into the support piece. You should drive them all the way into the hole to the back surface of the support piece. Be sure you have the notch facing up. You might want to round the outer edge of the dowel using some abrasive paper. It tends to enhance the appearance of the dowels.

[9] Trace the ends of the support piece onto the upper back side of the legs. This area needs to be cut out to hold the support piece. Refer to Project 1 for both procedures and drawings for this task.

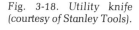
Fig. 3-18. Utility knife (courtesy of Stanley Tools).

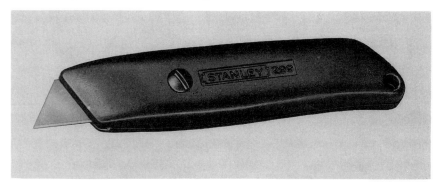

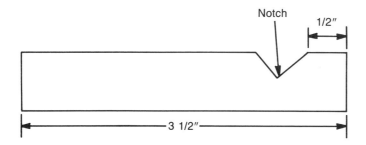

Notch

1/2"

3 1/2"

[10] Using glue and finishing nails, assemble the legs and the support piece. You can secure the leg and support assembly to the shelf top. Again, specific procedures for these various tasks are presented in Project 1.

Fig. 3-19. Dowel peg with notch.

PROJECT 3: PLATE SHELF

Although this project can be used as a narrow, standard shelf, it is designed to display and support plates (Fig. 3-20). A groove is cut or routed in the shelf top to allow plates to set in the groove and rest against the wall. It is an ideal shelf for displaying decorative or collectible plates. Project 4 is an alternative shelf design that provides a railing around the shelf top. That design provides more security from plates sliding off the shelf than is afforded by this project. For valuable plates, you might prefer the railing shelf design.

Because the Plate Shelf is made from 1-×-6 stock, you can hang it in places where a wider, 1-×-8 shelf will not fit. As you might recall, a 1-×-6 board is actually ¾ × 5½ inches. The width is important to remember as you plan the location of your shelf. I have made Plate Shelves in a wide range of lengths, including some that were 10 feet long. The design lends itself to running the

Fig. 3-20. Plate Shelf.

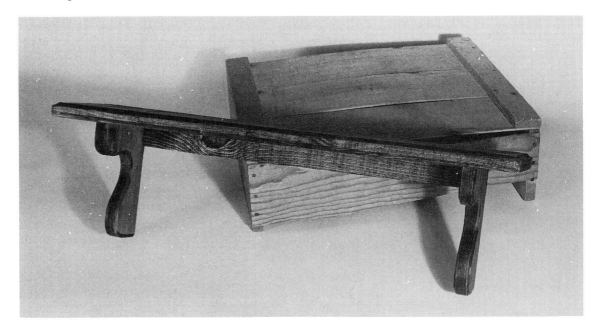

entire length of a wall to display various collectibles. The sample shelf will be a 1-×-6-×-24-inch project. This length is sufficient to be functional, but does not take up a lot of wall space. For a number of procedures for this project, I will refer you back to Project 1. After you make a few projects, you will be able to do the various tasks without referring to these earlier discussions.

[1] You will need enough 1-×-6 pine stock for a 24-inch-long shelf top, two legs, and a support piece. You might have enough scrap material around to make the legs and the support piece.

[2] As Fig. 3-21 indicates, the legs for this shelf design are very similar to the two previous shelf projects. There is, however, a dimensional difference between the two leg designs. Because the shelf top is from narrower stock, I usually make the legs smaller. The result is a better balanced appearance to the overall shelf. You might want to refer to Project 1 for a few ideas on other leg designs. Better yet, this is a good shelf for which to design your own leg shape. You might want to use the suggested leg dimensions for your design.

Whatever design you choose, review the discussion on patterns in Project 1. Prepare a pattern for the legs, then trace and cut. You also need to square one end of the board, then measure and cut the 24-inch-long shelf top.

Fig. 3-21. Leg for Plate Shelf.

[3] Cut a support piece that is 20 inches long and at least 1¼ inches wide. This length will enable the shelf top to overlap the legs by 2 inches.

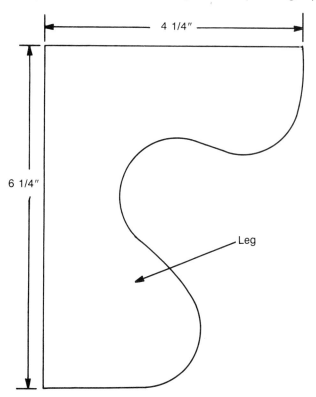

4 1/4"

6 1/4"

Leg

Review the discussion on support pieces and overlap in Project 1. If you want, you can rip the support piece to a thickness of ⅜ inch. A smaller Plate Shelf generally does not carry the weight that a standard or Shaker shelf would carry. Thus, if desired, the support piece can have less thickness. Sometimes a support shelf of full thickness on a small shelf distracts from its appearance. Use a band saw with a ½-inch-wide blade to rip or resaw the support piece.

[4] In order to keep the plates from sliding off the shelf, you must put a groove or ridge piece on the shelf top. There are a number of ways to make the groove in the shelf top's surface. Using a table-mounted router with a V-groove chamfering bit is probably the easiest. You also can make the groove using a ¼- or ⅜-inch-diameter round-nose router bit. Rout the plate groove at least 1 inch from the back edge of the shelf top and to a depth of at least ¼ inch. Although these measurements are approximations, you do not want to vary from them too much. Rout the groove the full length of the shelf top. You will need to use a fence or some kind of table guide on your router table. Select the least attractive side of the board for the top. Remember, you do not see the top of a shelf, only the bottom. Figure 3-22 shows a shelf top and the approximate placement of the plate groove.

If you do not have a router, you can cut the plate groove into the shelf top's surface with either a utility knife or a razor blade. You also will need a metal ruler or straightedge to use as a guide while cutting the groove.

Approximately 1 inch from the back edge, draw a straight line the entire length of the shelf top. This will be the back edge of the groove. Draw another line 1¼ inches from the back edge, running parallel to the first line. This second line will be the front edge of the plate groove. Depending upon how many plates you plan to display on the shelf, you might not need to cut the groove the entire length of the shelf top. The groove is only needed where plates will be placed.

Lay the shelf top on a hard surface. You want to cut the groove at an angle. This makes the cutting procedure considerably easier. Place the metal straightedge along one of the traced lines and cut. The cut only needs to be ¼ inch deep. Be certain you make the cut at an angle. When you make the second cut, also at an angle from the opposite side, the wood should pop

Fig. 3-22. Groove in top of the Plate Shelf.

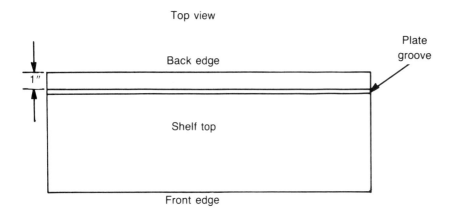

Top view

out of the groove. Take your time with this procedure and be extremely careful with the knife or blade. If a knot is in the way, cut up to it and then continue on the other side. You cannot cut through knots with a knife, so simply ignore them. All it will mean is that you will not be able to place a plate on the spot where the knot is. You can work around it as you set up your plate display. After you cut the groove, clean it up with abrasive paper.

Another, much simpler method for holding the plates from sliding is to use a strip of wood secured to the top surface of the shelf. You must do all routing of the various edges before you start this method. Find or cut a strip of wood about ¼ or ½ inch square and the length of the shelf top. Draw a line that is 1¼ inches from the back edge and runs the entire length of the shelf top. Place the strip on the back edge of the line. Using small brads (nails) and a spot of yellow glue, secure the piece along the penciled line.

If you can afford it, you can purchase a standard piece of trim for use as a strip. The wood strip will effectively prevent the plates from sliding when they are standing on edge. You can use thumbtacks to prevent the plates from rolling to the side.

[5] Rout the edges of the legs and shelf top. For these pieces, I use a ⅜- or ½-inch cove router bit. On the bottom edges of the shelf and the top back edge, I use a quarter round bit. I also use the quarter round on the back edges of the legs. Some of the edges should not be routed, including the support piece. Refer to Project 1 for a discussion on routing. If you do not have a router, you can sand the sharp edges with abrasive paper or lightly plane them. The proper use of abrasives can give a shelf a very countrylike appearance.

[6] Before you assemble any of the parts, sand all surfaces and some edges. After you are finished sanding, wipe off the dust from all surfaces before you assemble the shelf. If you routed the plate groove or cut it with a knife, be certain you sand any rough surfaces that remain in the groove.

[7] Using wood glue and finishing nails, assemble the legs and the support piece. Refer to Project 1 for assembling procedures. Glue and nail the shelf top to the leg and support assembly. You might, of course, prefer to use wood screws rather than finishing nails for the assembling process.

PROJECT 4: PLATE SHELF WITH RAILING

This project is a duplication of the basic Plate Shelf presented in Project 3. It has the added feature of a decorative railing that extends the length and on both sides of the shelf top (Fig. 3-23). The railing enhances the overall appearance of the piece. It gives the shelf a more formal look, and thus lends itself to use in rooms other than kitchens. It is especially appropriate as a dining room shelf. The railing also serves to protect plates and other collectibles from sliding or falling off the shelf. At least this design gives you more of a sense of security than the regular Plate Shelf.

You can make the shelf any length you desire. This design can extend the entire length of a wall or to a dimension that will accommodate only a few plates. The railing on the shelf, as will be discussed, can be either a plain

strip of wood or one that is decoratively routed. The railing support pieces are gallery rail spindles, and are available in a range of sizes and designs from a number of the mail-order suppliers listed in the Appendix.

Fig. 3-23. *Plate Shelf with Spindle Railings.*

If you are so inclined, you can cut standard ⅜- or ½-inch-diameter dowels to length and use them to support the shelf railing. You will find, however, that the commercial rail spindles are relatively inexpensive and make for a very attractive shelf railing. For this shelf design, spindles that are 1½ inches long, including their tenons, are more than adequate. Long spindles on a small shelf tend to make it look overly formal and gaudy. Our sample project will have dimensions of 1 × 6 × 15 inches. Although you might very well prefer a much longer project, these dimensions make for a very functional small shelf. This smaller design can be made in pairs and placed tastefully on a wall.

[1] Make the Plate Shelf that is 1 × 6 × 15 inches using the tasks and procedures presented in Project 3. Do the final sanding and routing on the shelf components. You can assemble the legs and the support piece, but do not attach them to the shelf top. Remember to rout or cut the plate groove in the top surface of the shelf top. You will do the final assembly of the shelf after the railing and spindles are in place.

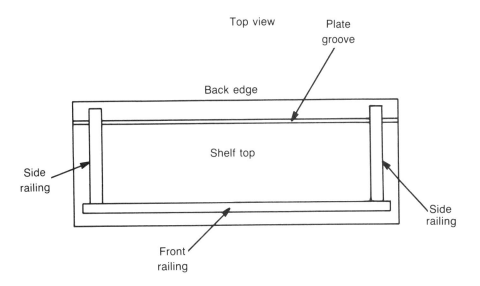

Top view

Plate groove

Back edge

Shelf top

Side railing

Side railing

Front railing

[2] If you prefer to make, rather than buy, the railings that surround the shelf top, cut them ¾ inch square. It is best to prepare the combined length of the railing front and sides in one piece. For a 15-inch-long shelf top, you will need a railing piece that is at least a combined length of 28 inches. It is easier to work with one long piece of railing rather than the three sections into which it eventually will be cut.

[3] After you have cut the railing piece to length, you can either rout or sand the various edges. A ⅜-inch round-over bit used on a table-mounted router is an effective way to roll the edges. If you decide to rout the railing, remove only a small amount of wood from the edges, especially from what will be the bottom edges of the railing. You need a surface that is sufficiently wide to accommodate a ⅜-inch-diameter hole for the spindle tenon. If you prefer a more formal design on the railing, use a small roman ogee router bit. If you do not have a router, use either a small plane or some abrasive paper to roll the edges of the railing.

[4] Next, cut the railing piece into three sections. It is necessary to cut one long piece for the front of the shelf and two smaller pieces for the sides. The 28-inch-long combined length of the railing piece should be of sufficient length for a 1-×-6-×-15-inch shelf. Figure 3-24 depicts the three railing pieces in relation to the shelf top. As the illustration indicates, the two side railings simply abut the front railing. If you prefer a fancier fitting railing, you can miter the corners and glue them together. Use small finishing nails to secure the mitered joints.

[5] The next task involves laying out the shelf top and railings for the placement of the railing spindles. For purposes of discussion, I will assume that you plan to use spindles that are 1½ inches long and have tenons that are ⅜ inch in diameter.

On the front edge of the shelf top, place a spindle every 3½ inches, beginning with the exact center of the shelf top. The sides usually have two spindles each, placed approximately 2½ inches apart. Figure 3-25 shows how to lay out the railings and the shelf top to mark the location of the drill holes for the spindle tenons.

As Fig. 3-25 indicates, place the railings, upside down, next to the shelf top. Using a ruler, measure and mark the locations of the tenon holes on the shelf top. The edge of the spindles should be at least ¼ inch from the shelf edge when in place. Remember that the diameter of the spindle body is greater than the diameter of the tenons. Allow for this difference when you are measuring for the placement of the spindle tenon in relation to the shelf top's edge. As indicated, the spindles on the front of the shelf should be approximately 3½ inches apart; the side spindles, 2½ inches apart.

After you have marked all the spindle tenon locations on the shelf surface, use a straightedge or ruler to transfer them to the bottom of the railing. Simply draw a straight line from the tenon mark on the shelf onto the bottom of the railing. Make an X in the exact center of the railing bottom where the tenon hole should be drilled. The mark should be at the center of the railing bottom.

[6] Using a ⅜-inch-diameter bit, preferably a wood bit, drill the tenon holes in the railings and the shelf top. Because the spindle tenons are usually ¼ inch long, drill the holes at least ⅜ inch deep. You would be wise to measure the actual length of the spindle tenons before you drill the holes. Take your time in drilling the holes and be certain they are made at the marked locations.

[7] Glue and tap the spindles into the three railings first. Spread a thin coat of wood glue on each tenon and tap it in place. If the tenons are a bit

Fig. 3-25. Spindle placement on the shelf and railings.

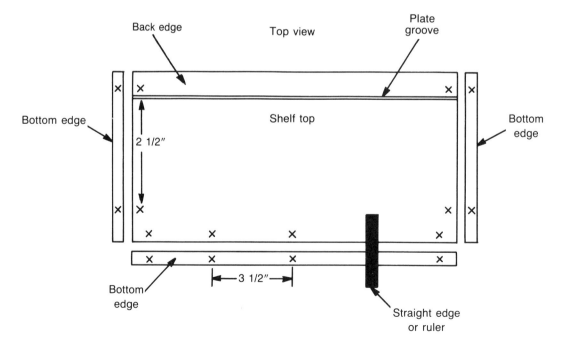

too large, you might need to wipe off the glue and sand them down using abrasive paper. Failure to have an exact fit can be a result of an undersized hole or an enlarged tenon diameter. You usually can solve the problem by sanding some wood from the tenon.

After you have glued the spindles into the railings, place glue on the other tenons and insert them into the holes in the shelf top. Using a small block of wood to protect the railing's surface, tap each tenon in place. Wipe off any excess glue that squeezes out of the tenon holes. Follow these procedures for all three railings.

[8] Assemble the shelf top to the leg and support assembly using glue and finishing nails. Refer to Project 1 for a discussion of these procedures.

PROJECT 5: SINGLE TOWEL BAR

This project is a rather simple design for a very functional towel bar for the bath or kitchen (Fig. 3-26). The unit consists of two support pieces with a dowel of any desired length penetrating the supports. The support pieces are designed with two countersunk drill holes for accommodating wood screws to secure the unit to the wall or a cabinet. What makes this design so functional is that you can vary the length of the dowel, depending upon the need or space available. Figure 3-27 presents a support piece and its approximate dimensions.

The support piece can be made from 1-×-4 pine, which is exactly 3½ inches wide. Generally I use ¾-inch-diameter dowels for the towel bar. This size dowel is less likely to bow under use, especially on a longer unit. It is also sturdier and offers more support for the towels. Although you no doubt

Fig. 3-26. Single Towel Bar.

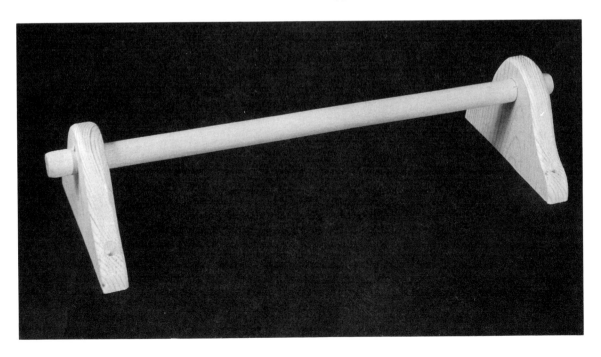

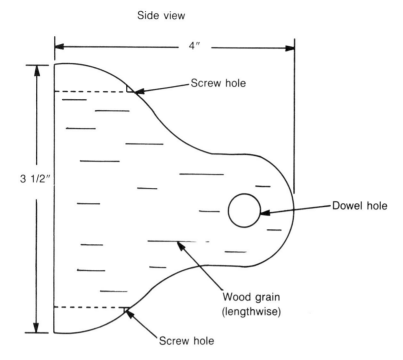

Side view

4"

Screw hole

3 1/2"

Dowel hole

Wood grain
(lengthwise)

Screw hole

Fig. 3-27. Towel Bar's support piece.

will want to design your project to your specific dimensional needs, the sample piece will be 15 inches long.

[1] Obtain sufficient 1-×-4 stock for the two support pieces. You can, of course, cut the support pieces from larger scraps that you have available. You also will need a length of ¾-inch-diameter dowel. Since most dowels are sold in 36-inch lengths, you will have sufficient dowel for two towel bars.

[2] Because you have two support pieces that are highly visible when placed on a wall, you want them to be identical. Therefore, you should make a pattern. You might prefer to make the support piece by drawing freehand on the wood's surface and then pattern the second one from it. Either way, the support pieces should be very similar in appearance and dimension. Be certain to pattern the support pieces with the wood grain, as pictured in Fig. 3-27, so the pieces will be stronger and less likely to break off under use. Pattern and cut the two support pieces.

[3] Drill a ¾-inch-diameter hole through each support piece, approximately ¾ inch in from the front edge of the support and centered on the support pieces. You want the drilled hole back from the front edge to maximize the strength of the wood. If the holes are too close to the edge, the wood could break out under use. Place a block of wood under the location of the holes during the drilling process. The block helps to prevent surface tear-out as the drill bit passes through the wood. Also, be certain to drill the two holes in the same location in the support pieces.

[4] Using a countersink drill bit or a standard ⅛-inch-diameter bit, drill

64

two holes through the top and bottom edges of each support piece. These holes will accommodate wood screws for attaching the towel bar to the wall or cabinet. Refer to Fig. 3-27 for the approximate location of these screw holes. Drill the holes at least ⅜ inch from the edges of the support pieces. You want to have as much wood as possible to support the screws and to hold the unit in place. If you are using a high-speed bit, make an indentation in the wood's surface at the bit's entry point to prevent the bit from skating around on the surface of the wood.

[5] After you have drilled all the holes, rout the edges of the support pieces. Do not rout the back edges that will be placed against the wall. A ⅜-inch round-over bit on a table-mounted router will do the job. You might prefer to sand the edges round rather than rout them. Either way, rounding the edges greatly enhances the appearance of the support pieces.

[6] Cut the ¾-inch-diameter dowel to a length of 15 inches. Using abrasive paper, round the sharp edges on both ends of the dowel. This procedure makes the dowel look more finished when it is in place. Slide the dowel through one of the drilled holes in a support piece to check for fit. If the dowel is too large, enlarge the drilled hole using abrasive paper, a round wood rasp, or a round file. Frequently, dowels are oversize in diameter when you buy them. It is a good practice to carefully measure their diameter before you purchase them. The drill bit also could be worn, thus making an undersized hole. Do not force the tight dowel into the drilled hole or you will split the support piece. You want a snug fit, but not one that is too tight. Using a range of abrasive papers, prepare all the surfaces for finishing.

[7] If the dowel fits too loosely in the support holes, you might want to place a touch of wood glue inside the drilled holes. You only need to place glue in one hole, but if you spread it in both, you will have a more secure dowel. You should allow the dowel to extend at least 1 inch beyond the outer surface of both support pieces. This design greatly enhances the overall appearance of the towel bar.

PROJECT 6: DOUBLE TOWEL BAR WITH SHELF

The Double Towel Bar with Shelf is a fine looking and very functional unit Fig. 3-28. It is an excellent piece for the bath, not only for hanging towels but also for making extra shelf space available. This project uses 1-×-8 stock and dowels that are ⅞ inch in diameter. Although you can use ¾-inch-diameter dowels, they are not as attractive on this large project. The small difference in diameter significantly affects the overall appearance.

Unlike the Single Towel Bar design, this unit has the dowels secured in ⅞-inch-diameter holes partially drilled into the inside walls of the legs. This procedure allows the dowels to roll in the holes as towels are pulled from them. Small screw hole buttons are placed in the outside leg surface opposite the internal dowel holes. These decorative buttons tend to break up the long leg surface and enhance the overall appearance of the project. Of necessity, the shelf employs a support piece so it can be firmly fastened to the wall.

Although I make this project 18 inches long, my preference is to build

it 24 inches long. You might want to modify this length in relation to your needs. To demonstrate how the project is made, however, I will use a length of 24 inches for the shelf top. Before you begin the various tasks, it will be helpful in your planning to see and know the dimensions of the legs. Figure 3-29 depicts one of the shelf legs with its dimensions.

Fig. 3-28. Double Towel Bar with Shelf.

[1] This project is made from 1-×-8 stock. You will need sufficient pine for the 24-inch-long shelf top and the two legs, each 11 inches long. Additionally, you need a 20-inch-long strip that is at least 1¼ inches wide for the support piece, and two dowels with ⅞-inch diameters and 36-inch lengths. You can use the extra ⅞-inch-diameter dowel pieces with one of the later projects.

[2] You might want to cut your support piece from a piece of 1 × 4 to minimize waste. Measure and cut the shelf top to a length of 24 inches.

[3] You would be well advised to make a pattern for preparing the legs. A sheet of construction paper is exactly 11 inches long, so you already have the length of the leg laid out. Refer to Fig. 3-29 for the other dimensions of the leg, along with its overall design. Mark the various dimensions of the leg on the construction paper. Make the scroll design freehand within these dimensions and cut out the pattern. While you are making the pattern, also measure and mark the exact location of the dowel holes. These dimensions are also given in Fig. 3-29.

Place the back edge of the pattern against an edge of the board and trace.

Be certain to cut the top edges of the legs square. You want a good, tight fit when they are secured to the bottom surface of the shelf top. You can cut the legs easily using a saber saw and a fine-toothed blade.

[4] Measure and cut the support piece to a length of 20 inches and a width of 1¼ inches. This length will enable the shelf top to overlap the legs by 2 inches on each side. Drill a ¼-inch-diameter hole 2 inches from each end of the support piece. Center the holes on the piece. These two holes will accommodate the screws or nails used to secure the shelf to the wall.

[5] Trace the butt end of the support piece onto the upper, back edge of each leg. You must cut out this area on each leg so the support piece can be secured to the legs. Refer to Project 1 for specific procedures. After you have traced the areas, cut them out using a saber or band saw.

[6] Examine the surfaces of each leg and decide on the best side. I put the best-looking side outward. Place your leg pattern on the inside surface

Fig. 3-29. Leg for the shelf.

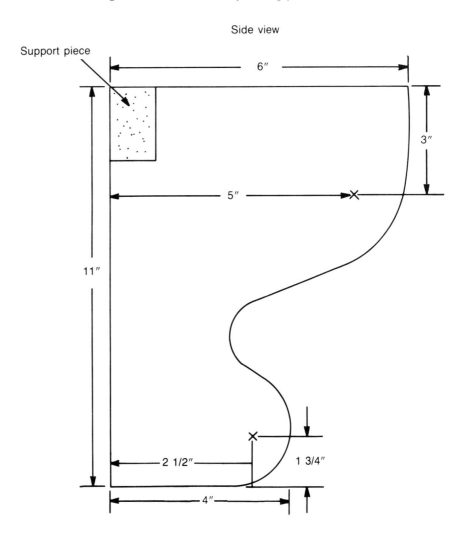

Side view

Support piece

6"

3"

5"

11"

2 1/2"

1 3/4"

4"

of a leg with the back and top edges flush with the leg edges. Mark the wood's surface by sticking a pencil through the points where you will place the two dowels. You should have identified these two locations when you made the pattern. If not, refer to Fig. 3-29 for the location of the dowels. Remember to use the pattern to mark the inside surface of both legs.

[7] Drill two holes ⅞ inch in diameter and ½ inch in depth into each leg at the points marked. Remember, the dowels on this design do not extend beyond the leg's surface. Instead, they roll in the holes drilled in the legs. You will need a bit or wood bore that is ⅞ inch in diameter. While you can make the holes using a hand electric drill, do it carefully. You do not want to drill through the leg. If you use a drill press, set the depth of cut before drilling. A forstner bit is excellent for drilling this type of hole. If the point of the drill bit penetrates through the outer surface of the leg, it is not a problem. This is the point where a small screw-hole button will be inserted into the surface of the leg after assembly.

[8] Cut the two ⅞-inch dowels into pieces 19 inches long. This length is critical to a proper fit when you assemble the various parts. Incidentally, you might want to think through why the dowels need to be exactly 19 inches long. Your pine legs are actually ¾ inch thick and your support piece is 20 inches long. You drilled holes that were ½ inch deep into each leg. This, of course, necessitates dowels that are 19 inches long for a perfect fit.

[9] Rout the edges of the legs and shelf top on a table-mounted router. I use a ⅜-inch cove bit for routing the top front and side edges of the shelf piece, as well as the front edges of the legs. I use a round-over bit for all other edges on both the shelf top and legs. Do not rout any of the edges that will fit against another part for assembly. Refer to Project 1 for routing procedures. If you do not have a router, roll the edges using abrasive paper or a small hand plane. You can produce a countrylike appearance by oversanding some areas of the shelf top and legs. Oversanding tends to give a piece a worn or used appearance.

[10] When you have finished routing, sand all the surfaces using abrasive paper. This project lends itself to using one of the small power pad sanders or even a large belt sander. Be certain you sand the surfaces with the grain of the wood. Begin with an 80-grit abrasive and work on through 150 or even 220 grit. The surface of all parts should be ready for the finishing process when the sanding is complete. Remove all the dust from those areas that will be glued during the assembly process.

[11] Now comes the somewhat difficult part of the project. Glue and nail one end of the support piece to one of the legs. Be certain the dowel holes are on the inside as you secure the support piece to the leg. Also, be certain that the end of the support piece is flush with the outside edge of the leg. Refer to Project 1 for the discussion on securing the support piece to the leg.

Next, lay the leg down flat on the outside surface with the support piece pointing upward. Place one of the dowels in a drilled hole in the leg surface and check for fit. If the dowel is too large, remove some of its surface using abrasive paper. You want it to fit loosely in the hole. Repeat the procedure with the second dowel. If you prefer the dowels to be stationary in their drilled holes, spread some glue on the wall of the two holes. As always, do not use too much glue.

Take the second leg and spread glue in the support piece cutout on the leg. Carefully place the leg on the dowels, allowing them to enter their respective holes. You might need to sand off some of the dowels' diameter to make them fit. Let the support piece slide into its cutout area on the back of the leg. Next, carefully turn over the entire unit and place the front edges of the legs on the surface. You need to nail the support piece to the second leg. If the dowels should fall out of their holes during this procedure, simply replace them and try again. You might want to get someone to assist you with these procedures.

[12] When you have assembled the legs, support piece, and dowels, set the unit upside down on the top edges of the legs. Make sure the top edges are square to the surface on which they are placed. If they are not square, carefully twist the entire assembly by holding one leg and pushing on the other. This procedure eventually should make the top edges of the legs square to the surface. The legs need to be square so that you can properly secure the shelf top to them. Allow the assembly to sit in this upside-down position until the glue is dry.

[13] After you have measured the shelf top for the proper overlay of 2 inches, use wood glue and finishing nails to secure the shelf top to the leg assembly. Refer to Project 1 for suggestions on this procedure. This is the final task in the assembly process and should be done with care. You want to have the shelf top properly placed and secured to the leg assembly.

[14] The final task is to drill ½-inch-diameter holes in the outer leg surface directly opposite the dowels. Stand the shelf on end for this procedure and use an electric drill and a ½-inch wood bit. These ½-inch holes will receive the tenon of the screw-hole buttons that should be placed on the outer leg walls. As indicated earlier, these buttons give the legs a more finished appearance. Without some type of decorative touch on the leg walls, they tend to look incomplete. The screw buttons add a nice finishing touch to the legs' outer surfaces (Fig. 3-30). Place a bit of wood glue on the button tenons and tap them in place.

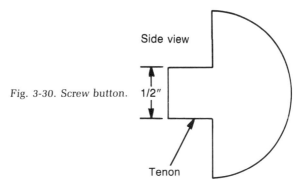

Side view

Fig. 3-30. Screw button.   1/2"

Tenon

PROJECT 7: PAPER TOWEL HOLDER

There are any number of possible designs for holding large rolls of paper towels. Some designs are functional, while others provide a shelf and decorative back for tole painting or carving. You might want to select a design that can be hung under kitchen cabinets. This type of design eliminates the need to have a unit occupying counter space. This project presents the under-the-counter design (Fig. 3-31). If desired, you also can attach it to a wall immediately under the cabinets. Either placement eliminates the need to have toweling take up space on already limited counter area. Figure 3-32 presents this functional paper towel holder, as well as its various dimensions. Although there is some opportunity to modify the dimensions of the unit, they are somewhat fixed by the measurements of a roll of toweling. Should you prefer to significantly modify the design, be certain to have a large roll of paper toweling available for making the necessary measurements.

[1] The towel holder is most efficiently made from 1-×-4 stock. You will need sufficient 4-inch-wide material for the two legs and the support piece. Recall that 1-×-4 pine is actually ¾ × 3½ inches. As Fig. 3-32 indicates, the towel holder is made to the actual width of the material. You may, of course, use wider stock. Simply saw it to the necessary dimensions.

Use ¾-inch-diameter dowel to hold the roll of paper. You also might prefer to use either a larger or smaller diameter dowel. A good practice is to use a dowel that corresponds to the diameter of a drill bit that you already have available. For example, if you only have a ½-inch-diameter drill bit, use a ½-inch-diameter dowel. Although the larger diameter dowels are preferable, smaller ones are certainly acceptable. This is one of the ways you can reduce your investment in tool accessories.

[2] Measure and cut the support piece to a length of 11½ inches and

Fig. 3-31. Paper Towel Holder.

70

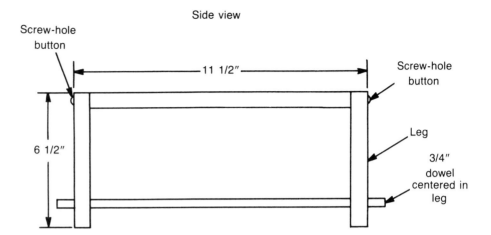

Side view

Screw-hole
button

11 1/2"

Screw-hole
button

6 1/2"

Leg

3/4"
dowel
centered in
leg

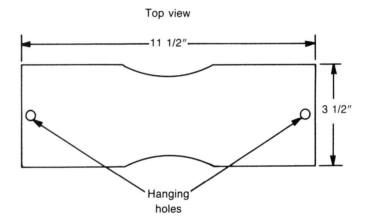

Top view

11 1/2"

3 1/2"

Hanging
holes

Fig. 3-32. Design of the Paper Towel Holder.

a width of 3½ inches. You will note in Fig. 3-32 that a decorative cut is made on each side of the support piece. You might want to make a similar cut or leave the support sides straight. Incidentally, the length of the support piece allows ¼ inch between both ends of the roll of towels and the legs. Paper towels seem to be made in a standard 11-inch length. Allowing an extra ¼ inch in length enables the towels to roll more easily for removal. The roll will not rub against the legs.

[3] Since the ends of the legs are rounded, you might want to make a pattern to ensure uniformity. An alternative approach is to design and cut one leg and then pattern the other from it. This procedure eliminates the need for making a paper pattern. You can cut the various pieces easily with a saber saw and a fine-toothed blade. You can make the round end of the legs using a coffee can or a similar item as a pattern. Cut the two legs to a length of 6½ inches and a width of 3½ inches. Although this length might seem somewhat long, it allows you to use some of the extra-large paper toweling

71

that is on the market. You might want to change the length of the legs in relation to the product you normally use.

[4] Drill two holes through the legs to accommodate the dowel. As indicated previously, I use a ¾-inch-diameter dowel for this project. Thus, you will need a wood bore or a bit that has a diameter of ¾ inch. Figure 3-33 presents the dimensions for placement and drilling of the dowel holes in the legs.

After you have measured and marked the location of the dowel holes on the legs, drill both holes. Place a scrap of wood under the legs during the drilling function to prevent tear-out. I place two ½-inch-diameter tenon screw-hole buttons on each side of the legs. (Fig. 3-33) These are false screw holes because the holder is assembled using wood glue and nails. The buttons add a decorative touch to the walls of the legs. You might, however, prefer to actually use wood screws for assembling the unit. In this case, use buttons to cover the screw heads. In any event, while you are drilling the dowel holes, also drill the tenon holes for the buttons. As indicated, the buttons need a ½-inch-diameter hole.

[5] The holder is secured to the wall or counter generally with screws.

Fig. 3-33. Leg for holder.

Side view

Screw-hole buttons
(1/2" tenon)

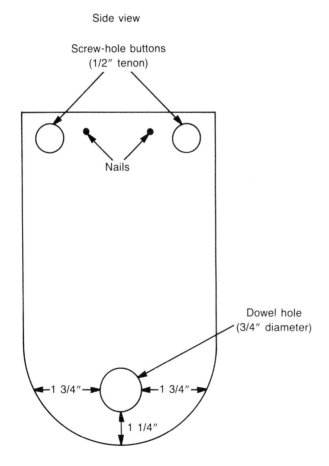

Nails

Dowel hole
(3/4" diameter)

←1 3/4"→   ←1 3/4"→

1 1/4"

72

Thus, you need to drill two holes through the support. Refer to Fig. 3-32 to get an idea of the approximate location of these hanging holes. You can either use a countersink drill or a ⅛- or ¼-inch high-speed bit to drill these two holes.

[6] Cut a ¾-inch-diameter dowel to an approximate length of 15 inches. This length will enable the dowel to extend beyond the legs by at least 1 inch. To determine the dowel length, add the length of the support piece, the thickness of the two legs, and the 1-inch extension on both sides of the dowel.

[7] Using a series of grits, sand all surfaces on the unit. You can round the various edges using either a round-over bit on a table-mounted router or a small hand plane or abrasive paper. Do not round over any of the various edges that will be joined together. You also should round the ends of the dowel to give it a more finished appearance. Remove all dust before assembling.

[8] Spread glue on the butt end of the support piece and nail a leg to it using finishing nails. Using wood glue and nails, secure the other leg to the support.

After the glue is dry, test the fit of the dowel. The dowel should fit snugly so that the paper towels will roll on the dowel. If the dowel is too tight, use abrasive paper, a round file, or rasp to carefully increase the diameter of the dowel holes. Continue the process until the dowel fits properly in both holes.

PROJECT 8: PAPER TOWEL HOLDER WITH SHELF AND DECORATIVE BACKING

This project is exactly the same as Project 7 only it has a scrolled decorative back piece (Fig. 3-34). If desired, you can glue the dowel in place and use the project for hand or dish towels. The significant difference between the previous towel holder and this one is that this project provides an area for tole painting. Figure 3-35 presents one possible configuration and approximate dimensions of the backing, you might want to explore a range of possible designs, varying both the dimensions and the amount of scrollwork.

One alternate design for the decorative backing is to include a small heart cutout (Fig. 3-36). Make a pattern of a heart and then trace it onto the backing. You can vary the size of the heart to meet your own design tastes.

[1] The project requires 1-×-6 stock for the shelf top, 1-×-6 stock for the back piece, and 1-×-4 material for the legs. You can rip the support piece from scrap. As with the previous towel holder design, a ¾-inch-diameter dowel is recommended. Material requirements are given in Fig. 3-35.

[2] Using 1-×-6 stock, measure and cut the shelf top to a length of 15 inches.

[3] Pattern or design the legs freehand to a length of 6½ inches and a width of 3½ inches. This width is, of course, the actual width of 1-×-4 material. As with many projects, to minimize sawing, design them around the actual width of standard pine lumber. Figure 3-37 depicts a leg, its dimensions, and the location of the dowel hole. As indicated, lay out the dowel toward

Fig. 3-34. Paper Towel Holder with Shelf and Decorative Backing.

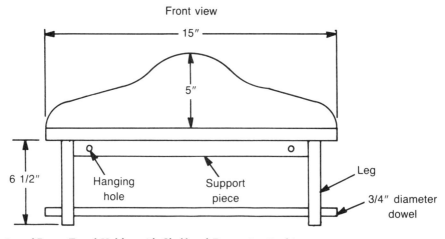

Front view

Fig. 3-35. Design of Paper Towel Holder with Shelf and Decorative Backing.

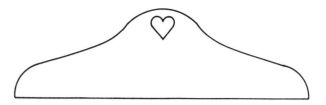

Fig. 3-36. Heart design for the decorative backing.

the front edge of the legs on this design. This placement prevents the toweling from rubbing on the support piece or, with larger rolls, on the wall.

[4] Drill ¾-inch-diameter holes through both legs.

[5] Measure and cut the support piece to a length of 13 inches. It should be at least 1¼ inches wide, cut from standard thickness pine. This support piece length will allow the shelf top to overlap the legs by 1 inch on each side. If you are curious, this length was arrived at by adding the 11½-inch length required by the roll of toweling and the ¾-inch thickness of the two legs. With a 15-inch-long shelf top, this leaves a 1-inch overlap on each side. I generally limit the overlap on this design to minimize the amount of wall space required for the unit. Of course, you might prefer a long shelf top with a greater overlap. Drill two hanging holes in the support piece.

[6] It is best to make a pattern for the back piece, especially if you decide on a more elaborate scroll design. You only need to make a pattern for half

Fig. 3-37. Leg for holder.

Side view

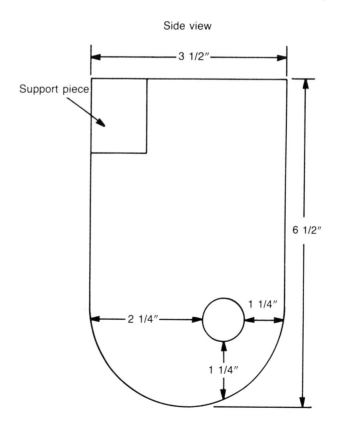

the length of the back piece. Trace the pattern on one half of the board, reverse the pattern, and trace the second half. Align the pattern at the exact center of the back piece. This type of patterning ensures that both sides will be exactly the same. It is also easier to do because you can make the pattern from one sheet of construction paper.

Cut the back piece to the necessary length. A saber saw with a fine-toothed blade is the ideal tool for making scroll cuts.

[7] If you desire a heart design, make a heart pattern. Then center and trace the pattern on the surface of the back piece. Drill a ¼-inch-diameter hole through the center of the pattern, insert the saber-saw or scroll-saw blade, and cut.

[8] Trace the butt end of the support piece onto the upper back surface of each leg. Refer to Fig. 3-37 for the correct location. Cut out the support area from both legs. A saber saw and fine-toothed blade works well for this procedure.

[9] If you have a table-mounted router, rout all edges using a ⅜-inch round-over or quarter-round bit. You might want to try a different edging bit for this design. I tend to use either a quarter-round or cove bit on most of the functional pine projects. There are a range of other decorative router bits that you might want to consider. Do not rout any edges that will be joined to another part during the assembly process. For example, do not rout the top edges of the legs because they will be attached to the bottom surface of the shelf top. You want to leave as much wood surface in place as possible. Also, routing in these areas distracts from the overall appearance of the project. If you do not have a router, use a small hand plane or abrasive paper to round the edges and corners.

[10] Cut a ¾-inch-diameter dowel to a length of 15 inches. This length will allow the dowel to extend beyond the surface of both legs by 1 inch. It also will match the shelf overlap.

[11] Using a range of abrasive papers, sand all the surfaces and edges to finishing readiness. It is much easier to do your sanding before the unit is assembled. You do, however, need to be careful with excess wood glue squeezing onto the newly sanded surfaces. Wipe off any excess glue using a warm, damp cloth.

[12] Assemble the support piece and legs using wood glue and finishing nails. Before you attach the shelf top to the leg assembly, you must secure the back piece to the shelf top with wood glue and finishing nails. The back edge of the shelf top and the back surface of the decorative back piece must be flush. Figure 3-38 shows this assembly.

[13] When the glue is dry, assemble the shelf top with its back piece to the leg assembly. Make sure there is a 1-inch overlap on both sides. Spread wood glue on the top edge of the support piece and the legs. Using finishing nails, secure the shelf top to the two legs. Since the back piece is secured to the shelf top, you will be unable to drive nails into the support piece. Clean off any excess glue.

[14] After you have assembled the unit, test the fit of the dowel in the

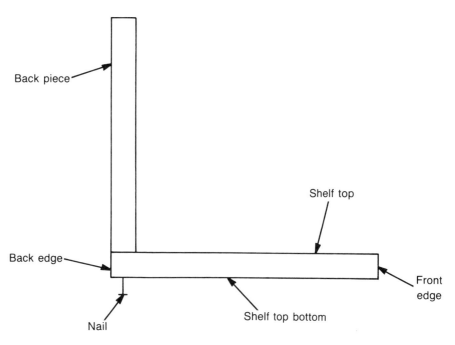

Side view

Back piece

Shelf top

Back edge

Front edge

Shelf top bottom

Nail

Fig. 3-38. Assembling the shelf top and back piece.

two leg holes. If necessary, widen the holes to accommodate the dowel. You want a snug, but not a tight, fit. It is best if the paper toweling rolls on the dowel. In this way, the dowel will not slip out of the leg hole during use. Refer to Chapter 4 for the finishing process.

PROJECT 9: TOILET TISSUE HOLDER WITH SHELF

This project is an extension of the double towel bar with shelf presented in Project 6. In fact, it is a companion piece for the bath. It is a functional tissue holder with a small shelf (Fig. 3-39). Although the shelf can be used for small items, it is added primarily to enhance the overall appearance of the design. You can secure the unit to a vanity or, if preferred, directly to a wall. Figure 3-40 indicates some of the important dimensions. Use a 7/8-inch-diameter dowel for this project. You can use scrap pieces of dowel from previous projects, if available.

By way of information, a standard roll of toilet tissue is approximately 4½ inches long. You need to allow a minimum of ⅛ inch on each side of the roll when you are measuring the length of the support piece. This allowance will permit free movement of the roll during use. For our sample project, the support piece should, therefore, be at least 6¼ inches long. Incidentally, I rip the support piece from standard stock to a thickness of ⅜ inch because it does not need to be full thickness.

[1] The two legs for the project can be made from 1-×-4 stock, but you

Fig. 3-39. Toilet Tissue Holder.

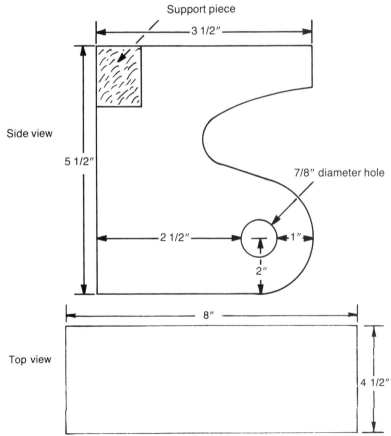

Support piece

3 1/2"

Side view

5 1/2"

7/8" diameter hole

Fig. 3-40. Design of the Toilet Tissue Holder.

2 1/2"

1"

2"

Top view

8"

4 1/2"

will need at least 1-×-6 material for the shelf top. As just indicated, you can cut the support piece from a scrap piece of pine. Measure and cut the shelf top piece to the dimensions given in Fig. 3-40.

[2] Design and make a pattern for the legs to the dimensions suggested in Fig. 3-40. You might want to duplicate the leg shape or redesign it to a configuration more to your liking. Using the pattern, trace and cut the two legs. Be certain to pattern and cut them with the grain. A saber saw with a fine-toothed blade will cut both the straight edge and the curves very effectively.

[3] Using the dimensions given in Fig. 3-40, lay out and drill the dowel holes in each leg. If you do not have a ⅞-inch-diameter bit, you might want to use ¾-inch-diameter dowels and a ¾-inch-diameter drill or wood bore. Remember to place a piece of scrap under each leg when you drill the holes to prevent tear-out of the surface as the drill bit exits the holes. After you have drilled the holes, cut a piece of dowel 8 inches long. The dowel should extend beyond the outer surface of the legs and match the overlap of the shelf top.

[4] Cut the support piece to a length of 6¼ inches. It should be approximately 1¼ inches wide. As indicated earlier, on this design I rip the support piece to a thickness of ⅜ inch. A piece this size can be ripped easily on a band saw with a 1-inch-wide blade. If you lack the capacity to resaw the piece, use its full thickness.

[5] After you have cut the support, drill screw holes through it approximately 1¼ inches from each end of the piece. The screw holes are used to secure the unit to a vanity surface or a wall.

[6] Trace and cut the support piece area in the back of both legs.

[7] Rout the various edges using a round-over bit and a table-mounted router, or roll the various edges using abrasive paper. Also, sand all the surfaces to a finishing readiness. Roll the ends of the dowel with abrasives. Refer to Project 1 for a discussion on table-mounted routing.

[8] Using wood glue and small finishing nails, assemble the support piece to the back of both legs. Refer to Project 1 for the various procedures of assembly. Secure the shelf top, using glue and nails, to the leg assembly. Using a nail punch, recess the heads of the finishing nails in the shelf top.

[9] Test the dowel for fit in the two leg holes. If it is too large, enlarge the holes slightly using abrasive paper or a round file or rasp. The dowel should fit snug, but you also should be able to remove it with ease.

PROJECT 10: JUG SHELF

Although primarily a decorative project, you can use the Jug Shelf (Fig. 3-41) as a small, functional display unit. The name seems to have emerged over time as a result of use. Very often, small jugs, either functional or decorative, were stored on this type of shelf. As you will discover, the project offers sufficient shelf area for displaying any number of small items. Additionally, its back, support surface provides an excellent area for tole painting.

The project is best made from 1-×-8 pine. The side pieces are more easily made from 1-×-4 material or scraps. Figure 3-42 presents the shape and various

Fig. 3-41. Jug Shelf.

dimensions of the back piece, as well as a side view of the project with some additional dimensions.

As you consider the project, you might want to redesign the neck area of the back piece. You can give it a scroll effect or some other more elaborate shape. I am inclined to more simple and straightforward lines, as indicated in Fig. 3-42. If you are so inclined, you also can modify the side pieces. Although their primary function is to provide support for the extending shelf piece, they are also decorative. Figure 3-43 presents the shelf piece and its dimensions. If you decide to modify the side pieces, be certain to apply any dimensional changes to the shelf.

[1] You will need sufficient 1-×-8 pine for the back piece and the shelf.

You can pattern and cut the two side pieces from 1-×-4 stock or possibly scraps.

[2] Make the back pieces' neck area from a pattern or design it freehand. The important thing is to have the curves even and the top of the neck in the center of the board. Prepare the back piece and saw it to dimension. You should find the midpoint of the board and drill a hanging hole in the lower portion of the neck. This shelf looks very attractive when hung on either an antique square or standard nail. Refer to Fig. 3-42 for the approximate location of the nail hole.

[3] Lay out the two side pieces and cut them to the dimensions given in Fig. 3-42. I tend to give these pieces some curved lines to enhance their appearance. You might want to make a pattern or simply design one piece and trace the other from it. Be certain of the measurements on the bottom section of the piece where it will be attached to the shelf side. You want a nice, clean fit because this is a highly visible area. A saber saw works fine for cutting the side pieces.

Fig. 3-42. Parts of the Jug Shelf.

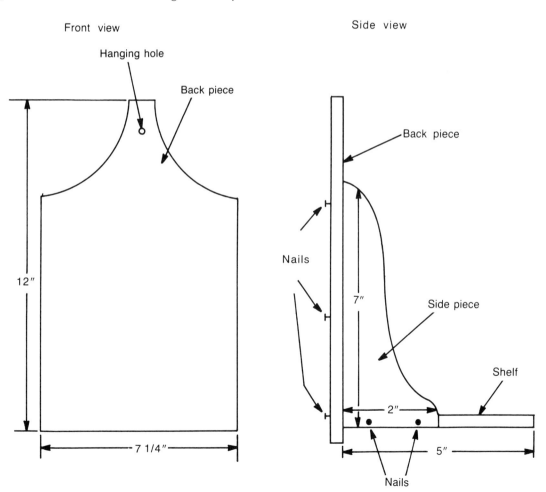

[4] Design and cut the shelf from 1-×-8 stock. You might want to make a pattern for this piece. It is important that the two areas where the side pieces will fit be cut to the same dimensions as the side pieces. Check the already cut side pieces to be certain of their exact dimensions. Figure 3-43 details the shelf piece and the areas that need to be removed for the side pieces.

[5] Rout the edges using a table-mounted router and a round-over bit, or sand the sharp edges to a slight roll. Do not rout or sand those edges that will abut another part during assembly, for example, the back edges of the shelf piece.

[6] When you have finished routing, sand all the surfaces and the routed edges to a finishing readiness. Remove all sanding dust from the various surfaces.

[7] Using wood glue and finishing nails, secure the side pieces to the shelf cutout areas. Refer to Fig. 3-42 for the placement of nails. Spread glue on the back edges of the side pieces and the back edge of the shelf. Align this assembly on the front surface of the back piece and press into place. Allow the glue to dry partially. Carefully turn the entire assembly over and place the front edges of the side pieces on a hard surface. Drive finishing nails from the rear surface of the back piece into both side pieces. Refer to Fig. 3-42

Fig. 3-43. Jug Shelf piece.

Top view

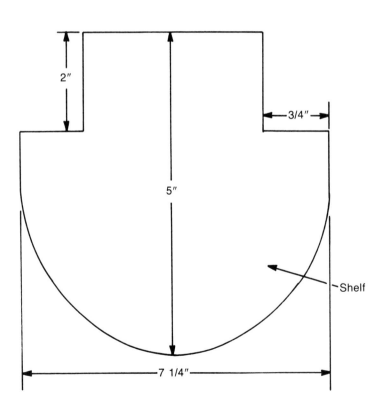

for possible locations for the nails. Be certain the side pieces and the shelf do not move out of position during the nailing process.

[8] If the side pieces do not pull up snug against the surface of the back piece, you might want to clamp the assembly with bar clamps. Place scrap pieces of wood between the surfaces of the side pieces and the clamps. If you do not protect the pieces with scraps, the clamps will mark the surfaces.

[9] Allow the assembly to dry. Wipe off any excess glue that squeezes out from the various joints.

PROJECT 11: SCRAP MIRRORS

Although the name of this project might be somewhat misleading, these mirrors (Fig. 3-44) are in fact made from scrap material. Being the kind of woodworker who tends to save scrap material, I am always exploring with different ways to use it. Some years back I began making these small mirrors from pine scraps. The interesting part of these mirrors is that you can make them in a wide variety of sizes and shapes. Most of them are quite small and the actual mirror in them is often only 2 inches in diameter. They are, however, extremely decorative, especially when they are grouped together on a wall.

In addition to using scrap pine, I also use pieces of mirror glass cut from larger projects. They are often more than adequate in size for using in scrap mirror frames. Once you begin making these small projects, you might want to simply cut into a standard 12-×-12-inch panel of mirror glass, which is available at most hardware stores. The project can be great fun and an opportunity to explore with some different frame designs.

Fig. 3-44. Scrap Mirrors.

Since the shapes of the frames are totally freestyle, dimensions are not an issue with this project. The designs in Fig. 3-44 are some examples of what is possible with a minimum of design work.

[1] Using scrap material, design and cut a number of frames. Although you might want to make the frames similar, I would suggest you consider making each one different. The frames can be easily cut using a saber saw.

[2] To make the mirror area in the center of the frame, use large multispur bits or even spade bits. I usually make the mirror hole from 1 to 1½ inches in diameter. If you have a drill press, you also can use a circle cutter to make a variety of different-sized holes.

If you want to make a mirror area that is not round, use a saber saw. Do not limit the mirror area to only one shape. Try some different shapes to house the mirror. Drill or cut the mirror area from the frames.

[3] Rout both the front and the back edges of the frame with a round-over bit. Also rout the front edge of the mirror area. Do not, however, rout the back edge of the mirror area with the round-over bit.

You might want to consider a cove or ogee router bit on some of the frames. These bits will give you some different effects on the edges of the projects. The small scrap mirrors are good projects to experiment with various router bits and note their effect on the edges.

[4] You will need to recess an area on the back surface of the frame to hold the mirror glass. To rout this area, use a ¾-inch-diameter straight-face router bit. This type of bit is also referred to as a *mortise bit*. Set the bit to a cutting depth of no more than ⅛ inch. This depth is adequate for accommodating the mirror glass. Also, if the depth of cut is any deeper, the procedure becomes dangerous.

To rout the mirror area in the back of the frame, place the frame hole over the revolving bit. While you are holding the frame very tight, move it into the bit and rout out an area all around the mirror hole. The routed area does not need to be perfect. It only needs to be large enough to hold a piece of mirror glass. I often make the recess almost square to simplify cutting the piece of mirror that will fit into the recess. Take your time with this routing procedure and practice effective safety procedures. The recessed area and the piece of mirror both will be covered with a piece of construction paper, so do not be concerned about the quality of the recess. Its edges can be rough and of any shape. The important thing is to make the recess large enough to hold a piece of mirror glass that will totally cover the drilled hole in the center of the frame.

[5] Sand the edges and surfaces of the frame to finishing readiness. Be certain to lightly sand the mirror hole in the frame. Finish the frame before you glue the mirror in place.

[6] If you are not inclined to cut your own mirror glass, no doubt a local glass shop will be very accommodating. If you take your frame to them, most shops will cut the mirror glass to an exact fit. I hope, however, that you at least try cutting your own mirrors.

Fig. 3-45. Standard Glass Cutter.

Before you begin the process of cutting the mirror glass, you need a pattern of the area and its recess. You will need to cut the glass so that it fits neatly into the recessed area. To make a pattern for the glass, trace an outline of the frame pattern on a piece of construction paper. Measure the width of the recess that you made. In most instances, this area will be ¼ inch wide. Using a ruler, make a series of marks on the pattern paper that are ¼ inch away from the edge of the traced pattern. You should make the marks all around the pattern. The procedure is to draw a new pattern by connecting these various marks with a pencil. Cut the new pattern from the construction paper and test it for fit in the recessed area of the frame. If it is too tight, remove some paper from the edge. It is better to have it a bit too small than too large. This pattern will be the exact size of the mirror glass needed for the frame.

Using a felt-tipped pen, trace the mirror pattern on the reflecting surface of a panel. Use a fine-point pen and make the traced line dark enough so that it is easy to see and follow. It is best to place the pattern near one edge of the mirror panel to minimize waste.

To cut the mirror glass, you need a standard glass cutter and a steel edge ruler (Fig. 3-45). Place a drop of household oil on the small wheel on the front of the cutter so that it rotates with ease. Every now and then, repeat this step.

[7] To cut glass, hold the cutter firmly in your hand and run the wheel over the line or area you want to cut. The wheel lightly scores the surface of the glass and makes it possible to separate the glass along the scored line. You must use the cutter with both pressure and confidence. Only one firm pass should be made with the cutter along the marked line.

It is interesting to note how many individuals seem afraid to cut glass or mirror glass. This fear seems more related to breaking the glass than cutting themselves. For what it is worth, fear not, Mirror glass is relatively inexpensive and it is no great loss if you break a piece or cut it wrong. The chances of cutting yourself are very remote, at least if you are somewhat careful. After you score a few pieces and then separate them, you will find that glass cutting is really quite fun. It is interesting to see the various angles that can be cut. Take a piece of mirror glass and make some practice cuts and then separate the pieces. As with anything else, you will need to practice the procedure a few times. Waste some mirror on yourself. Consider it an investment in learning.

Before you begin to cut the traced pattern, separate the glass panel. Place the metal ruler near the edge of the traced pattern. While you are holding the cutter firmly in your hand and at a slight angle, run the wheel down the glass while keeping the edge of the cutter against the ruler. Keep the pressure constant on the wheel. Place the scored line over the edge of a board or your workbench. While holding one part firmly against the surface, press down on the other part of the mirror. It should neatly separate along the scored line. Do not be afraid to give it some good, quick pressure. It is important that the scored line be directly over the edge of the surface of the board or bench. Save the extra piece for your next mirror project.

Incidentally, when you are cutting glass, be certain the area under the glass is flat and clean. You want the glass to lay perfectly flat against the surface when you are cutting. Also, remove any glass particles that remain from earlier glass cutting. These small particles can scratch the black coating on the back of the mirror panel. Scratches can be seen from the reflecting side of the mirror.

To cut the traced pattern on the panel, the glass cutter needs to score along the inside edge of the traced line. You should score only one-half of the pattern with each pass of the cutter. Place the cutter wheel at the top edge of the pattern and, while applying pressure, slowly follow the traced line down to the bottom of the pattern. Turn the panel around and repeat the process on the other side of the pattern. Do not try to separate the pieces yet.

[8] In examining the glass cutter, you no doubt noticed two or three small grooves in the midsection of the cutter. These grooves are used for separating pieces of scored glass and also for chipping glass off the edges. Note that the grooves are of different widths. These widths are designed to fit over glass of different thicknesses. In addition to these grooves, note how the end of the glass cutter handle is made into a partial ball. This weighted end is used to tap along the scored line to make separating the glass easier. You should not tap on the piece you are cutting. Tap only on the waste side of the scored line.

While holding the scored pattern in one hand and holding the glass over the surface, tap along the scored lines. Next, place over the edge of the glass the groove of the cutter that best fits. Twist the glass cutter. This procedure should immediately separate a portion of the glass that surrounds the pattern. Continue this procedure until all the excess glass is removed from the pattern. You can chip off any small, sharp edges that remain on the pattern by using the cutter groove. If you break the pattern during these procedures, simply start over.

[9] Place the mirror in the recessed area of the frame and check for fit. If it is too large, using the cutter groove, chip away at the edges of the glass until it does fit. Take your time and keep chipping until you have a good-fitting mirror.

[10] Do not glue the mirror in place until after you have finished the frame's surface with whatever products you plan to use. To glue the mirror in place, use white glue. Spread small dabs of glue along the mirror edge and the wall of the recess. Allow the glue to dry. To cover the mirror and its recess, I measure and cut a piece of construction paper that will cover the entire back of the frame. Spread glue along the edge of the paper and press it in place. If you cover the hanging hole with the paper, simply punch a hole in the paper to expose the nail hole for hanging.

PROJECT 12: HEART MIRROR

This project presents an opportunity to make a mirror that is quite different. Although the basic heart design is not unusual, the inclusion of a heart-shaped mirror in its center is certainly different (Fig. 3-46). Not only is the Heart Mirror an attractive piece to make, it also demonstrates procedures that you can use

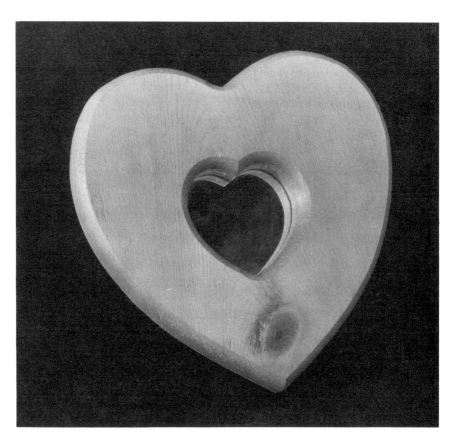

with other designs. The shape within a shape is an interesting and challenging approach to making mirrors.

Although you can make the project with almost any dimensions desired, Fig. 3-47 presents a relatively small design. Since the mirror is primarily a decorative piece, I am inclined to make it somewhat smaller than when I make a functional mirror. Even if I increase the frame's size, I still tend to keep the internal heart design quite small. You might, of course, prefer a larger internal heart mirror that can serve as a functional unit. Do some planning and design work in relation to where you want to hang the mirror. These explorations should help you decide on an appropriate size.

Another advantage to making the project small is that you can use scrap lumber. As was demonstrated in Project 11, there are endless ways to design and craft mirror frames from scraps. The small Heart Mirror would cluster very well with a collection of the Scrap Mirrors. Do not rule out the use of scraps for the project, including scrap pieces of mirror glass.

[1] To make the project to the dimensions suggested in Fig. 3-47, you need a piece of 1 × 6 that is at least 6 inches long. Recall that a 1-×-6 board is 5½ inches wide. Cut the material to length.

[2] If you are good at drawing a heart design freehand, you will not

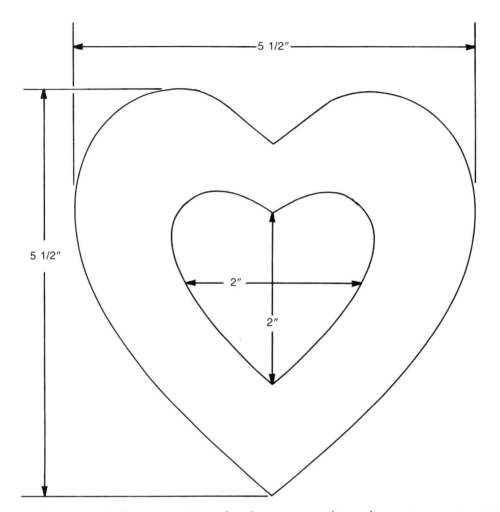

need a pattern for the project. Most of us, however, need to make a pattern.

To make a heart pattern, simply fold a piece of construction paper in half. Mark the length of the heart design along the folded edge. Also, mark the midpoint of the length. Next, extend a line from the folded edge, along the midpoint, to half the width of the design. For the sample project, you would make a mark that is 2¾ inches from the folded edge. Within these marks, draw a half section of a heart. The folded edge will be the center of the heart when the paper is unfolded. Using scissors, cut out, along the pencil line, the half heart. Open the paper and you should have a perfect heart.

[3] Trace the heart pattern, with the grain, on the length of 1 × 6. Using a saber saw, cut out the design.

[4] You will want to make a pattern for the small, internal heart that holds the mirror. Refer to Fig. 3-47 for the approximate dimensions of the heart. Use the same pattern procedures as just presented for the previous task. When you have made the pattern, trace it on the exact center of the larger heart frame.

Fig. 3-47. Design of the Heart Mirror.

88

[5] To cut out the internal heart design, drill a ¼-inch-diameter hole inside the pattern. Place the saber saw's blade through the hole and cut out the design. Take your time so that you have nice, clean edges on the heart. Portions of the heart can be somewhat difficult to cut. Think through your saw cuts before you make them.

[6] Drill a ¼-inch-diameter hole in the top back surface of the heart. This hole is for hanging the mirror. Be certain the hanging hole is centered.

[7] Using a round-over bit and a table-mounted router, rout both edges of the heart frame. Rout only the front edge of the internal heart.

[8] You will need to make a recess in the back surface to hold the piece of mirror glass. The procedure for routing this recess is presented in Project 11. Note also in that project the procedures and references for cutting mirror glass with a glass cutter. Rout and prepare the glass according to these instructions.

[9] Sand the entire surface and all edges to a finishing readiness. As indicated in Project 11, do not glue the mirror in the recess until the frame has been finished. Refer to Chapter 4 for some ideas, products, and methods on finishing. Glue a piece of construction paper on the back surface after you have finished the frame's surface and glued the mirror in place.

PROJECT 13: MIRROR SHELF

This project combines both a functional mirror and a shelf area for displaying decorative items (Fig. 3-48). It is a very attractive and functional design that can be hung in almost any room. The shelf is placed in such a way that items displayed on it reflect in the mirror. It makes for an interesting effect. It is also worth noting that the mirror in the project is of a size that can be used as a functional mirror.

This project requires a rather detailed pattern for the back piece of the unit. It is the type of pattern that can be made using the folded paper procedures discussed in Project 12. In addition to a frame pattern, I also make a pattern for the mirror area and the small shelf. You can draw the shelf's support piece freehand onto a board's surface. Although this might seem like a great deal of pattern work, the finished project is well worth the effort. As suggested earlier, patterns greatly simplify and enhance the appearance of most projects.

Although there is not a great deal of unused surface on the project, if you are a creative tole painter, you no doubt will find some areas on which to paint. You also might want to modify the dimensions to allow more surface for painting. If you are planning to tole-paint the project, do some design work prior to beginning the actual project. Figure 3-49 presents the Mirror Shelf and some of its dimensions.

[1] To ensure that you have sufficient material for the project, you will need at least 30 feet of 1 × 8. This length allows sufficient wood for the back piece, shelf, and support. Recall that a 1-×-8 board is 7¼ inches wide. This project maximizes this width to eliminate waste. You will, however, need to reduce the width of the small shelf.

[2] Cut the back piece of the project to a length of 17 inches. This will allow you some additional length to make patterning and cutting somewhat easier. While you are sawing, cut the small shelf board to a length of 5½ inches. Do not cut the support board at this point. You might decide to make it from a piece of scrap.

[3] You will need to make patterns for the various components of the project. You will need to tape together two pieces of construction paper to make the 16½-inch-long pattern for the back piece. To simplify the patterning process, it is best to make one pattern for the back piece and a separate pattern for the mirror area.

You will find it easier to make a pattern for this project if you fold the construction paper in half. Measure and draw the outline of the back piece on the folded paper. You will, of course, be drawing only half of the actual piece. Refer to Fig. 3-49 for the various dimensions of the back piece. Figure 3-50 depicts how the pattern will appear after it has been drawn on the folded construction paper. Using scissors, cut out the pattern and open it to full width.

Fig. 3-48. Mirror Shelf.

You also will need to make a pattern for the mirror in the back piece. It is best to use the folded-paper method for this pattern. Be certain to round the corners on the pattern and to prepare the pattern to the dimensions given in Fig. 3-49. You will find that this mirror area pattern also will be helpful when it is time to cut the actual mirror glass. You will, however, need to add to its dimensions.

While you are making your patterns, also make one for the shelf that extends from the back piece. Figure 3-51 presents an outline of the shelf, along with its dimensions. Use the folded-paper method to make the pattern. You might, of course, prefer designing and cutting the shelf without benefit of a pattern.

You can lay out and cut the support piece in Fig. 3-52 freehand, or you can use a pattern. I am always inclined to make and use patterns. Given the size of the support piece, you might prefer to simply saw it from a piece of

Fig. 3-49. Design of the Mirror Shelf.

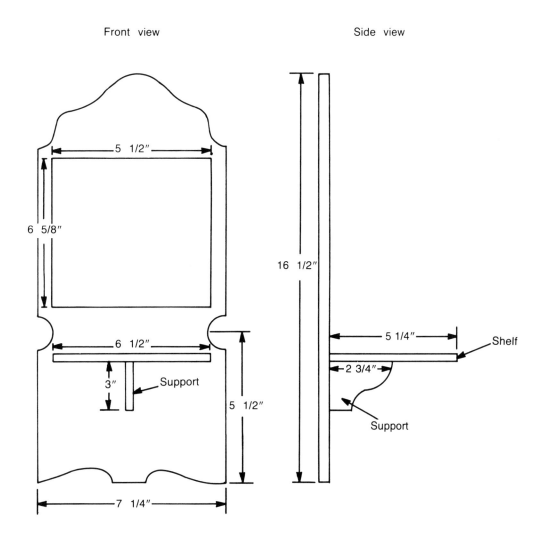

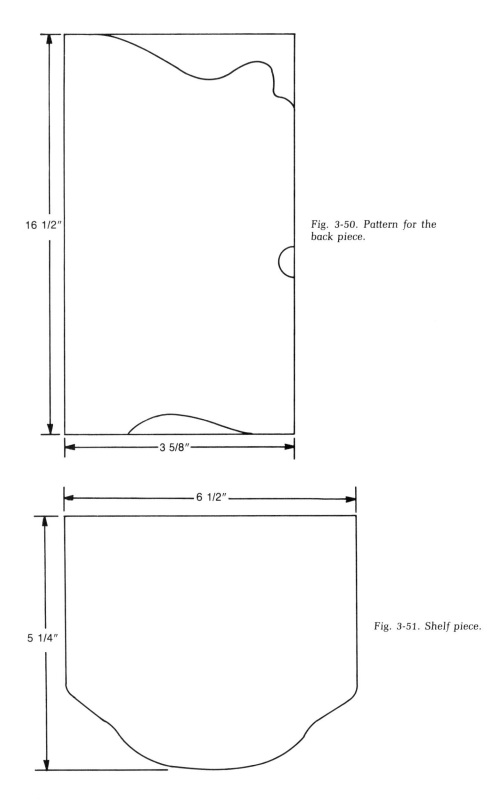

16 1/2"

3 5/8"

Fig. 3-50. Pattern for the
back piece.

6 1/2"

5 1/4"

Fig. 3-51. Shelf piece.

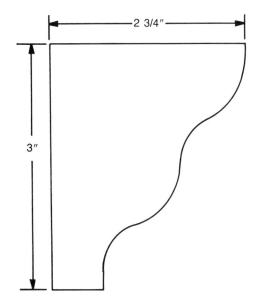

Fig. 3-52. Support bracket.

2 3/4"

3"

scrap without making a pattern. Be certain to check the suggested dimensions for the piece.

[3] Using the pattern for the back piece, trace it on the 17-inch-long piece of 1 × 8 that you cut earlier. Using a saber saw and a fine-toothed blade, cut the back piece from the board. Take your time with this function and saw carefully along the patterned lines.

[4] Center the pattern of the mirror area on the cutout back piece and trace. Be certain the pattern is properly centered. Refer to Fig. 3-48 for the location of the mirror area on the back piece. Drill a ¼-inch-diameter hole inside the traced area into which you can slip the saber saw's blade to begin the cut. Carefully saw out the mirror area, being especially careful on the rounded corners. You want good, straight edges on all sides and four rounded corners that match. It is critical to the overall appearance of the project that this area be cut as precisely as possible. When in place, the mirror tends to expose any edges or corners that are poorly sawed.

[5] Trace the shelf piece on the 5½-inch-long piece of stock that you cut earlier. Place a side edge of the pattern flush with one edge of the board to eliminate one cut and leave a good straight edge. Trace the pattern so that the wood grain runs lengthwise from the front edge to the back edge of the shelf. Using a saber saw, cut the shelf piece as traced. You also should prepare the small support piece using either a pattern or the suggested dimensions.

[6] Rout the outside edges of the frame, as well as the top edge of the shelf piece, using a cove bit on a table-mounted router, unless you prefer a different edge profile. Round the front edges of the mirror area and all other edges, including the support piece, with a round-over router bit. Do not rout the back edges of the mirror area, the back edges of the shelf piece, or the back and top edges of the support piece. Think through the routing function before you begin.

[7] In order for the mirror glass to be recessed into the back surface of the back piece, you must use a rabbeting bit on your router. Refer to Project 11 before proceeding. It is important that you do not attempt to rout too deep of a recess in one pass with the rabbeting bit. Rout the mirror recess.

[8] Sand all surfaces and edges to finishing readiness. Be certain you sand with the wood grain on the various parts. Leave the edges that will abut other parts sharp. This is also a good time to drill a ¼-inch-diameter hanging hole in the upper, back surface of the back piece. Drill the hole at a slight angle so that you can hang the project on a nail. Be careful not to drill through the back piece.

[9] Secure the shelf to the back piece using wood glue and small finishing nails. Before you begin this procedure, check the location of the shelf piece in Fig. 3-48. As you will note, it is placed just below the two small cutout areas on the edges of the back piece. It is a good practice to measure and mark for the location of the shelf piece. You can measure either from the bottom edge of the mirror area or from the two outer edges on the bottom of the back piece. This procedure will assist you in securing the shelf piece so that it is straight.

Spread glue on the back edge of the shelf piece and place it against the front surface of the back piece. Be certain to place it along the premarked locations. Press the shelf in place and allow the glue to partially dry.

Since nailing the shelf to the back piece is rather awkward, I allow the glue to dry sufficiently so that I can turn the entire piece over and nail it. The glue tends to hold the shelf to the back piece as the assembly is turned over. Rest the front edge of the shelf on a hard surface during the nailing function. Be certain to place and drive the nails so that they will end at approximately the middle of the back edge of the shelf piece.

As indicated, this procedure is somewhat awkward. On occasion, the shelf piece might fall off prior to being nailed. It is difficult to hold the two pieces together and nail at the same time. You might want someone to hold the assembly for you while you nail. Be certain to wipe away any excess glue.

[10] Spread glue on the top and back edge of the support piece and place it against the bottom surface of the shelf and the front surface of the back piece. Refer to Fig. 3-49 for the placement of the support piece. Drive small finishing nails at an angle through the support piece and into the shelf and back piece. Be certain the nails are small enough and placed at an angle so that they do not penetrate the surface of the back piece and shelf. Using a nail punch, tap the nails in the support piece slightly under the wood's surface. Wipe off any glue that squeezed out during the nailing function. Make sure you remove all glue from the various surfaces. As indicated earlier, stains used in finishing will not take where glue remains on the wood's surface.

[11] The final task is to measure and cut the mirror glass so that it will fit neatly into the routed recess. The pattern for the mirror area can assist you in laying out the mirror glass for cutting. Measure the width of the routed recess and add this measurement onto all four sides of the pattern. You can do this procedure while the pattern is laying on a piece of mirror glass. Sim-

ply mark the added dimensions onto the glass around the pattern. You also can use these marks when you are cutting the mirror glass.

For a discussion on cutting glass, refer to Project 11. First cut the corners on the mirror glass straight. Then, use the chipper groove on the glass cutter to chip each corner round. With some practice, you also can cut the corners round using the glass cutter. Take your time with this procedure so that you do not ruin a piece of glass. If you do, remember that glass is not all that expensive. With practice, you will learn to cut glass with relative ease.

PROJECT 14: FLOWERPOT DROP

The Flowerpot Drop is similar in design to Project 10. It is designed, however, to hold a 4-inch-diameter clay flowerpot in its shelf area (Fig. 3-53). In addition to holding a plant, the project also provides considerable surface for tole painting. It offers both a function and the opportunity to enhance it with a variety of painted designs.

The length of the back piece on this project is shorter than the one on the Jug Shelf. Because the flowerpot extends downward from the 4-inch-diameter hole, it does not need the length of the Jug Shelf. Figure 3-54 presents the back piece of the design, along with its various dimensions. You also will

Fig. 3-53. Flowerpot Drop.

note that the top portion of the back piece is designed quite differently than in Project 10. Either design is acceptable. You might prefer to design the top section of the back piece in a way more to your liking. For example, you might want to include some decorative scrollwork. You also might prefer the neck design presented in Project 10 over the one detailed in Fig. 3-54.

As you might guess, the back piece is made from 1-×-8 stock. Recall that a 1-×-8 board is actually ¾ inch thick and 7¼ inches wide. This width is, of course, the actual width of the back piece in this project. This type of planning and design work can eliminate a great deal of unnecessary sawing and also minimize waste. Figure 3-55 presents a side view of the Flowerpot Drop with the various dimensions.

Although the various parts and the assembling of the Flowerpot Drop are essentially the same as in Project 10, the dimensions for the project are significantly different. Figure 3-56 presents a top view of the Pot Drop shelf with the hole for accommodating the 4-inch-diameter flowerpot. The edges of the flowerpot or its tapered side wall support the pot on the edges of the shelf hole.

Fig. 3-54. Pot Drop back piece.

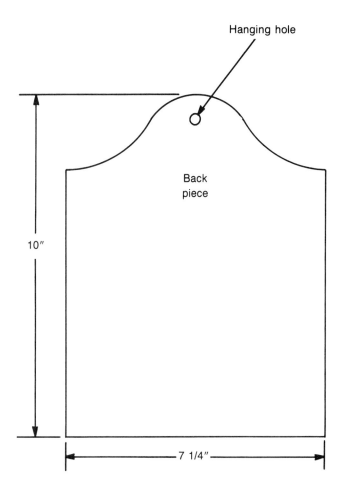

Hanging hole

Back piece

10"

7 1/4"

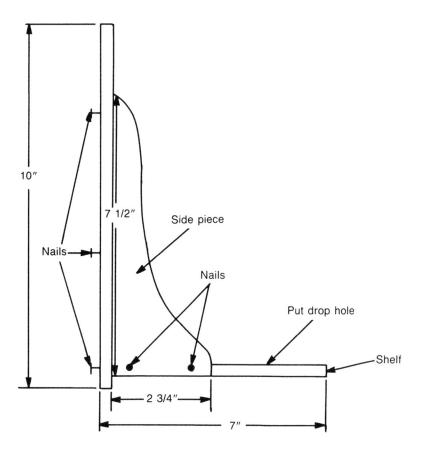

Fig. 3-55. Side View of the
Flowerpot Drop.

[1] Measure, design, and cut the back piece from 1-×-8 pine. You might want to design and make a pattern for the top section of the back. It is important to the overall appearance of the project that the curved areas on the back be somewhat uniform. Uniformity is best accomplished through the use of a pattern.

[2] After you have designed and cut the back piece, drill a hanging hole in the upper center of the back piece. You can secure the Pot Drop to a surface using either a nail or a screw that penetrates this drilled hole.

[3] Design the two side pieces using the dimensions presented in Flg. 3-55. It is important to prepare the bottom of the side pieces to the suggested width. They need to fit neatly into the cutout areas of the shelf piece. Cut the side pieces using a saber saw and a fine-toothed blade. A saber saw is an effective tool for cutting all the parts for this project, including the 4-inch-diameter hole in the shelf piece.

Be certain that you have good, straight edges on the back portion of the two side pieces. It is best to lay them out on the board so that the back portion is the edge of the board. In this way, you will be assured of a straight edge that will fit tightly and neatly against the front surface of the back piece.

[4] Using the dimensions in Fig. 3-56, prepare the shelf piece. Make

97

Top view

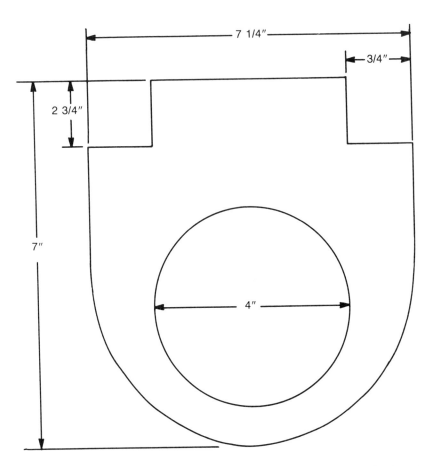

Fig. 3-56. *Shelf Top for the Flowerpot Drop.*

a pattern for the 4-inch-diameter hole using a compass. Be certain that the hole pattern is centered on the shelf piece. To cut the hole using a saber saw, drill a ¼-inch-diameter hole through the inside area of the pattern. Insert the blade of the saber saw through the hole and begin cutting. Take your time with the sawing function so that you have a neat, perfectly round hole.

Another option for making the hole is to use a circle cutter mounted in your drill press. (Refer to Chapter 2.) Set the cutter to make a 4-inch-diameter hole and proceed. Be certain you clamp the board to the drill-press table before you make the cut. If the board is not clamped, the circle cutter will grab the board and spin it around.

[5] Rout or sand all the edges, including the pot hole. Do not round over any of the edges that will abut other parts during assembly. For example, do not rout or sand the back edges of the side pieces.

[6] Sand all surfaces and routed edges in preparation for finishing. Remove the sanding dust prior to assembly.

[7] Assemble the shelf using the same procedures presented in Project

10. Be certain to remove any excess glue that might squeeze out of the joints during assembly.

PROJECT 15: SMALL DECORATIVE SHELF

This project is designed to display small decorative items (Fig. 3-57). It is also a design that presents a surface for tole painting or some other type of embellishment. The two legs, unlike previous shelf designs, are secured directly to the shelf top and do not require a support piece. Because the entire design is made from 1-×-4 stock, you easily can make it to any desired length with minimal investment in material. It is an economical shelf, but yet one that can be readily displayed in any room. The various devices for hanging this type of shelf are presented in Chapter 4, or you can simply drill holes through the decorative back piece.

The shelf design also can be made without the decorative backing. If the decorative piece is not attached to the shelf top, the width of the shelf increases to 3½ inches, the full width of a 1 × 4. You might want to consider this option as you plan for the project. In part, you should base your decision on the planned use for the shelf.

If desired, you can rout or cut a trench into the shelf top's surface to support the edge of a small plate. The shelf makes for an excellent mechanism to display small decorative plates. Refer to Project 3 for a detailed discussion on the preparation of plate shelves. Figure 3-58 presents both a leg and the overall view of the project, along with dimensions.

Fig. 3-57. Small Decorative Shelf.

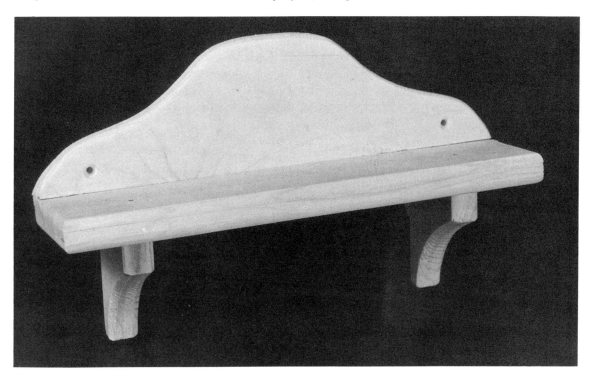

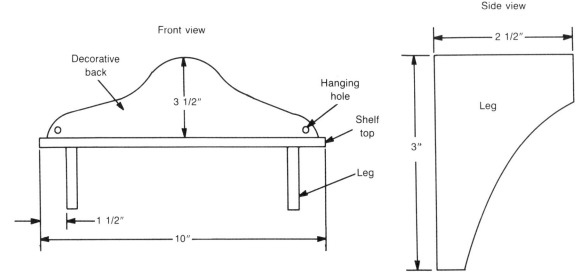

Front view

Decorative
back

Hanging
hole

3 1/2"

Shelf
top

Leg

Leg

2 1/2"

3"

1 1/2"

10"

Fig. 3-58. Design of the
Small Decorative Shelf.

[1] Measure and cut the shelf top to a length of 10 inches from standard 1-×-4 pine stock. Also cut the backing piece to a 10-inch length. You might want to design a pattern to duplicate the decorative backing that is presented in Fig. 3-58. To ensure uniformity, you can use a half-pattern approach. Make a pattern that is exactly 5 inches long. Trace half the decorative backing, using the pattern, on one-half of the board. Reverse the pattern and trace the other half.

You might prefer something a bit more elaborate than the backing design presented. You can increase the width of the back piece easily by using wider stock. For example, you might want to make it from 1-×-6 stock. If you have a band saw, you might also want to rip or resaw the ¾-inch-thick stock down to a thickness of ⅜ inch. Ripping will give you a thinner backing, but it also will give you more shelf surface. Trace and cut the backing piece using a saber saw.

[2] Pattern and cut the two legs to the dimensions suggested in Fig. 3-58. The leg design presented is rather basic, and you can improve it if desired. You might want to review some of the optional leg designs presented with Project 1. Better yet, try your hand at designing a set of legs more to your liking. Do the design work with construction paper and then transfer it to the wood.

[3] Rout or sand all exposed edges. A round-over bit with a table-mounted router gives a nice effect. Do not rout off too much of the edges. For a brief discussion of the routing function, refer to Project 1. Remember also not to rout or sand any of the edges that join another part of the project, for example, the bottom edges of the backing piece. Think through the assembly process before you rout the edges.

[4] When routing is complete, lightly sand all routed edges and the various parts' surfaces. Use a range of abrasive grits to prepare the surfaces for finishing.

[5] Using wood glue and finishing nails, attach the decorative backing to the top, back edge of the shelf top. Drive the nails from the bottom of the shelf top into the bottom edge of the backing piece. You must complete this step before you attach the legs.

[6] Glue and nail the legs to the bottom of the shelf. Be certain the legs are placed an equal distance from the edges of the shelf top. I usually allow a 1½-inch overlap on this design. Drive the nails from the top surface of the shelf into the legs. If you plan to make a groove for supporting plates, do so prior to attaching the back piece to the shelf.

PROJECT 16: T SHELF

Although this project can have a decorative backing for tole painting or some other type of embellishment, it also makes for an excellent small, functional shelf (Fig. 3-59). It is one of those designs that can be varied both in length and shape. The shelf top can be made into a standard rectangle or, using wider stock, made into a half-moon shape. Either way, the shelf is an attractive unit for use in any room.

The project employs but one leg, thus its name. You can design the leg rather simply, or, especially with the half-moon top, you can give it some elaborate scrollwork. It is a fun shelf to make and one that is relatively easy and quick to do. Although I will suggest some standard dimensions for the sample shelf, you might want to measure and custom-design your own projects. There are a number of hanging options for this type of shelf that

Fig. 3-59. T Shelf.

are presented in Chapter 4. Figure 3-60 presents a number of design options for the shelf top. Also note the various suggested dimensions.

Although I generally make the shelf top from 1-×-4 stock, for a larger half-moon design, you will need to increase your wood requirements. To minimize costs, designs using the 4-inch-wide stock are best. Our sample shelf will be made with the rectangle shelf top presented in Fig. 3-60.

Figure 3-61 presents a number of leg designs, along with some suggested dimensions. As you might guess, the larger the shelf top, the larger the leg that is required. The leg is needed not only for purposes of support but, more importantly, for appearance. The size of the leg thus should be in relation to the size of the shelf top, or the entire shelf will appear a bit odd. Proportion is important to this design.

[1] Using 1-×-4 pine stock, measure and cut the shelf top to a length of 6 inches. Since the rectangle shelf top design will be used for our sample shelf, the standard 3½-inch width is appropriate. If you are planning a decorative back piece, cut it to the same length and pattern the desired scrollwork on it. If you want the shelf top to support a plate, rout or cut a groove into the surface. Refer to Project 3 for procedures.

[2] Design, pattern, and cut the leg. Figure 3-61 gives some ideas on leg designs, as well as dimensions. This is another project where you can design a leg to suit your tastes. An advantage with this project is that you need only one leg, so you can make it as fancy as you want. You will not need to duplicate it as in most other shelf designs. Explore some ideas and shapes using construction paper. You also can vary the suggested dimensions.

[3] Rout or sand the edges on both the shelf top and the leg. You might want to use a roman ogee or some other router bit that will give you more elaborate looking edges. Do not rout any of the edges that will join to other parts.

[4] After you have finished routing, sand the routed edges and the various surfaces using a range of abrasive grits. Remove all the sanding dust from the various parts prior to beginning the assembly process.

[5] Place the leg at the bottom center of the shelf top. Its back edge must be flush with the bottom back edge of the shelf top. Spread wood glue on the top edge of the leg. Drive finishing nails through the top surface of the shelf top into the leg. Allow the glue to dry. Be certain to remove any excess glue from the various surfaces.

[6] If you included a decorative backing in the design, spread glue on its bottom edge and nail the shelf top to it. Drive the nails from the bottom of the shelf top into the bottom edge of the backing. Be certain the back edges of both parts are flush.

PROJECT 17: SHAKER PEG TOWEL HOLDER

A rather simple design, but one that can provide a wide range of functions, is the one-peg holder (Fig. 3-62). A single Shaker peg is secured into either a plain or decorative backing. Depending upon where the unit is placed, it

Top view

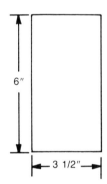

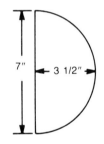

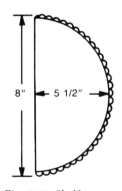

Fig. 3-60. Shelf tops.

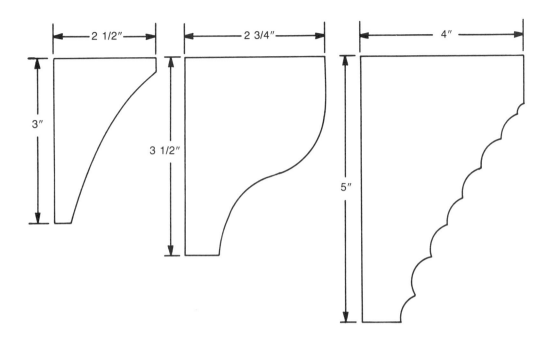

Fig. 3-61. Shelf legs.

can be used for a towel holder, robe holder, or any number of other functions. With a small cup screw secured into the backing, it can be attached to the side of a vanity to hold both a hair dryer and a hand towel. A small-diameter dowel can be used in place of the cup screw.

Fig. 3-62. Shaker Peg Tow-el Holder.

Although the backing for this project is rather small, it does provide sufficient area for tole painting or other type of enhancement. You might, of

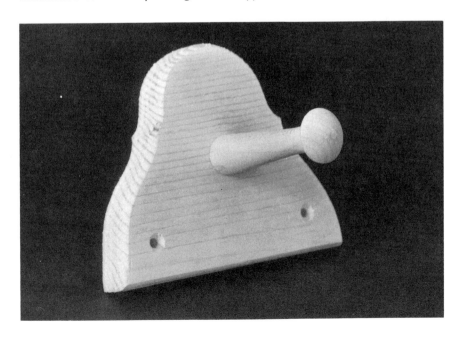

course, increase its size to allow for more painting surface. Also, you can design the backing with various scroll cuts to enhance its overall appearance. These more decorative backings make for a more interesting piece for painting.

I prefer making this project using a commercial Shaker peg; however, you can use a ½-inch-diameter dowel. Sources for Shaker pegs are listed in the Appendix. Figure 3-63 presents two basic designs and their dimensions for the backing part of the project.

Fig. 3-63. Design of the Shaker Peg Towel Holder.

Front view

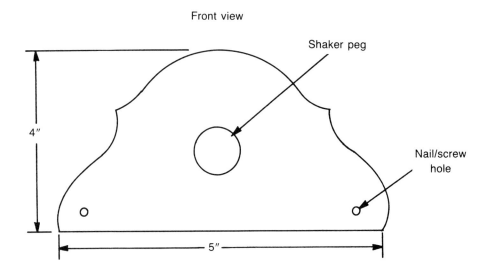

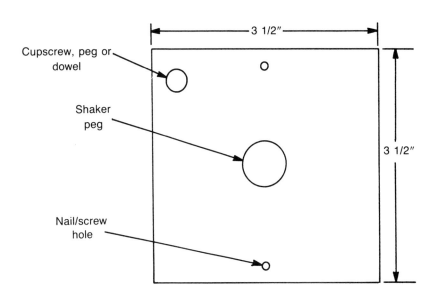

[1] Depending upon both the size and design of the backing, prepare and cut it as desired. One of the designs presented in Fig. 3-63 can easily be made from standard 1-×-4 stock. You might want to measure the area to which you plan to secure the project, or at least have a general idea of the dimensions you want before you saw the unit. These dimensions might depend upon your planned use for the project, as well as a specific design you would like to paint on the backing.

[2] Measure and mark the location for the Shaker peg or dowel. I place the peg in the approximate center of the backing piece. Using a ½-inch-diameter bit, drill the peg tenon hole through the backing. Always drill the hole from the front surface to the back. In this way, if tear-out does result from drilling, it will be on the back surface. Incidentally, most commercial Shaker pegs have a ½-inch-tapered tenon, which is why you should use a ½-inch-diameter bit.

[3] In order for the holder to be held securely to the wall, vanity, or other surface, you should make two nail/screw holes through the backing. Drill the holes through the surface, where they will give the backing the most support when secured. Any project using pegs should be securely attached to a surface. Chapter 4 provides both information and assistance on some of the various methods best used for hanging projects.

[4] Rout or sand the face edges of the backing. Also sand the surface and edge to finishing readiness.

[5] Spread glue on the Shaker peg's tenon and drive it into the ½-inch-diameter hole. Wipe off any excess glue. If the fit is not tight, squeeze some glue on the tenon edge from the back. Allow the glue to dry.

PROJECT 18: PLAIN SHAKER PEG BOARD

The Plain Shaker Peg Board (Fig. 3-64) is one of the most functional ones that you can make. It lends itself to placement in any room in the house and can be used to hang or display an assortment of items. Made from 1-×-4 stock, it can be made to any length desired. It also can be made to accommodate any number of Shaker pegs that you want or need.

Although you can make pegs from ½-inch-diameter or larger dowels, it is best to purchase the commercial Shaker pegs. The pegs are ingeniously designed with a tapered tenon that is firmly secured into a ½-inch-diameter hole. The decorative peg is flared at the front end to prevent items from sliding off it.

As suggested, this project design is for a very functional wall unit. Although you might want to paint on the project, your painting could be covered up by whatever is hung on the pegs.

Although I have made Shaker Peg Boards in lengths ranging from 1 to 8 feet, it is best to design them to the actual length you need. In addition to measuring for length, you also should decide how many pegs will be used. For example, if the pegs will hold coffee mugs, you can place the pegs approximately 3 inches apart. If you plan to hang coats on the pegs, you might want them to be at least 5 inches apart. Do some measuring to determine

Fig. 3-64. *Plain Shaker Peg Board.*

the approximate area needed for each item to be hung on a peg. Then, measure and place the pegs accordingly.

It is best to secure the Shaker Peg Board to the wall or some other surface. You will need to drill holes, appropriately placed, along the length of the board. Peg boards that are constantly in use need to be secured or they will continually fall off regular wall hangers. Incidentally, the commercial Shaker pegs are usually made from birch or hard maple, which are very strong woods. The pegs will not break off under intensive use. More often, the unit would pull from the wall before a peg would break.

[1] Determine the length of the board required and cut it from 1-×-4 pine. When you are selecting your stock, be certain the board is reasonably straight.

[2] After deciding upon the distance needed between the pegs, measure and mark the location for each peg. You want the pegs to be centered on the board and in perfect alignment with one another.

[3] The commercial Shaker pegs, as indicated, have a ½-inch-diameter tapered tenon. Thus, you must drill a ½-inch-diameter hole through the board at each peg location. Place a scrap piece under the board when you are drilling to prevent tear-out from the bit. Also, mark and drill from the front surface of the board.

[4] Rout or sand the front edges of the board. Sand the surface and the edges with abrasive paper. You want to bring the board to finishing readiness.

[5] Spread wood glue lightly on the tenon wall of the pegs and drive

them into the drilled holes. If you are using a steel hammer, place a scrap of wood between the hammer head and the peg's surface when driving it into place to prevent the hammer from marring the surface of the peg. If you are using a wooden mallet, this problem is eliminated. Be certain to remove any glue that squeezes out onto the surface of the board when the peg is driven into place. If the pegs do not fit tightly, spread some glue in the exit holes over the tenon ends on the back of the board.

PROJECT 19: SMALL OPEN CABINET

The small open cabinet (Fig. 3-65) is ideal for hanging on almost any wall to display collectibles or other items. Its size is small enough so that it can be easily hung in almost any room or hallway in the house. At the same time, it has enough shelf space that it can accommodate a range of items.

The project is also well suited to serve as a functional storage cabinet in the bath or any other room where hanging storage space is needed. Given the width and depth of the cabinet, it lends itself to being hung on a wall

Fig. 3-65. Small Open Cabinet.

behind a door. It is one of those functional designs that can maximize the dead space often found on walls behind doors.

You might want to increase the size of the project cabinet significantly. You can easily custom-design and craft it to fit a particular location. Also, you can design it to hold and display items of a particular size. You might want to make the cabinet to a size that will display some type of collection. For example, I make this same style open cabinet using 1-×-6 stock, increasing its length to 24 inches and its height to 18 inches. Using various widths of stock and different dimensions, you can make the cabinet to any size desired.

The size of your cabinet should be determined by where you plan to hang the project and how you will use it. The procedures for making any open cabinet are essentially the same, regardless of size. Figure 3-66 presents the project cabinet, along with its dimensions. Do some planning and design work before you begin the project. Design and make the cabinet to meet your specific needs.

[1] Use 1-×-4 stock. If you do not have a band saw to rip ¼-inch-thick strips for the back boards of the cabinet, you will need to use ¼-inch-thick or thinner plywood. A band saw also will be useful in resawing the shelves and the side pieces of the cabinet. If you do not have a band saw, you can

Fig. 3-66. Design of the Small Open Cabinet.

Front view

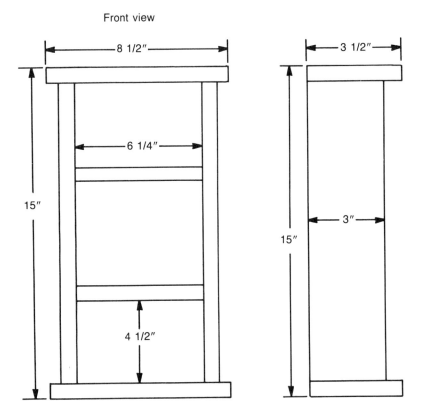

use other methods to accomplish particular tasks. There are always ways to improvise when you are making a project. The lack of a particular tool should not stand in your way.

To make the cabinet frame and shelves, you will need a minimum of 5 feet of standard 1-×-4 stock. This does not include the material required for the back boards or board of the cabinet.

[2] Using Fig. 3-66 and its dimensions as a guide, measure and cut the various pieces. After you have cut the two side pieces to the appropriate length, rip them to a width of 3 inches. If a band saw is not available, use a saber saw with its guide attachment to rip the side pieces to width.

[3] Rip the two shelves to a width of 2½ inches. This width allows the shelves to be slightly set in from the edges of the side pieces.

If you have a band saw, rip the two shelves to a thickness of ½ inch. This shelf thickness tends to enhance the overall appearance of the cabinet. It also makes for a bit more space between the shelves. As indicated earlier, if you do not have a band saw, simply leave the shelves at their standard ¾-inch thickness.

[4] Rout selected edges on all the cabinet pieces using a round-over bit and a table-mounted router. Because you will rout a groove in the back bottom edges of the end pieces and the inside edges of the side pieces, do not round over these areas. The grooves will hold the backing strips or the plywood.

Using a round-over router bit, rout the front two edges of both shelves. Rout the front edges and one back edge on both side pieces. On the two end pieces, rout the two front edges, the end edges, and one edge on the back of each piece. Do not rout edges that will make contact with another surface when assembled.

Using a rabbeting bit in a table-mounted router, rout a groove in the back edges of the end and side pieces. Rout the groove on those edges that were not routed earlier. The groove should be ¼ inch deep or less. The depth of the grooves is determined by the thickness of the back strips or plywood that you plan to use. Although ¼-inch-thick strips or plywood make for a strong cabinet, a ⅛-inch thickness is acceptable. Do not attempt to rout too deep at a single pass with a rabbeting bit. Make shallow cuts and a number of passes. The rabbeting bit can be dangerous and should be used with care.

[5] Using a range of abrasive grits, sand all edges and surfaces to finishing readiness. After the cabinet is assembled, sanding is almost impossible, so do a complete and thorough sanding while you have the opportunity.

[6] Join together the sides and end pieces first. Use wood glue and finishing nails for this procedure. When you are assembling the parts, it is best to have a surface where the various pieces can be placed on their back edges. To ensure the side pieces are assembled in such a way that the shelves will fit snugly between them, use the shelf pieces as a guide. Place the shelf pieces, unsecured, between the side pieces while you are nailing the side pieces to one of the ends. This procedure is somewhat awkward, but is worth

the effort. The distance between the side pieces needs to be exact so that you will have good-fitting shelves.

Spread wood glue on the ends of the side pieces, place a shelf between them, and set the end piece in place. Be certain the rabbeted grooves are on the inside. You also should place the end piece so that it extends an equal distance on both sides of the side pieces. While you are abutting the side pieces against something, drive finishing nails through the end piece and into the side pieces. Use two finishing nails on each side piece. Reverse the process and attach the second end piece to the sides. Remember to use one of the shelves to separate the side pieces during this procedure.

When assembling, it is important that the back edges of the end and side pieces are flush. The unit will be flush it you lay it on its back when you assemble it. Take your time with the assembly procedures. Think through each step before you drive in any nails. Remember to have the routed grooves of each part on the inside edge. They will hold the back support pieces, so it is important that you place them correctly. Wipe away any excess glue that was forced onto the surfaces.

[7   Using a nail punch, drive the heads of the finishing nails slightly under the surface of the end pieces.

[8] To secure the two shelves inside the cabinet frame, cut two pieces of 1-×-4-inch scrap material to a length of 4½ inches. Place these two pieces, with the cabinet standing upright, against the inside surfaces of the side pieces. Then place the shelf on top of these pieces for nailing. This is an effective way to properly place and secure both shelves inside the frame. While the shelf is held in place on the scrap pieces, turn the cabinet on its side for nailing. The back edge of the shelf should be flush with the edge of the rabbeted grooves. The back support boards will fit tightly against the back edge of the shelf.

While the shelf is resting on the two pieces of scrap, drive two finishing nails through the side piece and into the end of the shelf. Be certain to place the nails properly so that they will enter the center portion of the shelf. Repeat the process on the other end of the shelf.

To secure the second shelf, repeat the procedures at the other end of the cabinet assembly.

The scrap pieces that are used for guides in the placement of the shelves can be any desired length. If you plan to place an item of a particular height on a shelf, measure and cut the scrap pieces accordingly. You can vary the distance between shelves and the two ends by making scrap guides of different lengths. Using guides is a very effective way of placing shelves in a cabinet. It also ensures that the shelves will be level when in place.

[9] Prepare the back support pieces or plywood. As indicated, if you have a band saw, it is relatively easy to rip stock to the necessary thickness. The strips should be at least 1 inch wide. The final strip will be a different width, depending upon how much area remains after the 1-inch-wide strips are in place. The strips should, of course, run up and down on the back surface of the cabinet.

Measure the length of the strips needed from the top edges of the routed grooves in the end pieces. The measured width between the side pieces will determine the number of strips needed. Secure the strips in place using wood glue and wire brads driven into the routed groove.

If you are using plywood, measure the inside of the back edges and cut a piece to these dimensions. Remember to measure to the edges of the routed grooves so that you can secure the plywood in place. You also can use wood glue and brads to secure the plywood in place. Be certain that the grain of the plywood is running up and down when you place it in the cabinet.

To simplify finishing the cabinet, I usually do not secure the strips or plywood in place until everything has been finished. This is especially true if you plan to stain the various parts of the cabinet. Staining is much easier if the back board or strips are not in place. Nail and glue the back board after the finishing process is complete.

PROJECT 20: CANDLE BOX

Although originally designed by some Early American homeowner to actually be used for holding candles, this project (Fig. 3-67) is probably better used today for decoration. The design makes it an ideal piece for tole painting. Depending upon possible planned uses, the box can be hung or placed on a flat surface. It also can be varied significantly in size. If you plan to use the box for a particular purpose, design it accordingly. You might prefer a much larger box, especially if you plan to tole-paint a design on it.

Fig. 3-67. Candle Box.

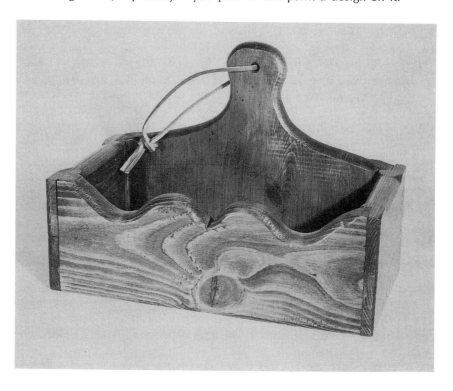

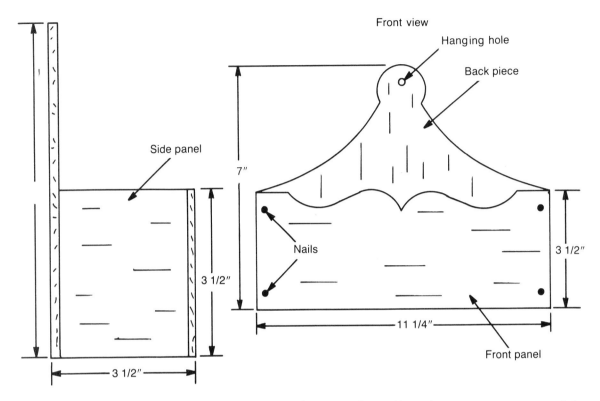

Side view

Front view

Hanging hole

Back piece

Side panel

7"

Nails

3 1/2"

3 1/2"

11 1/4"

3 1/2"

Front panel

You can make the project using a combination of 1-×-4 and 1-×-12 stock. In part, the actual material required will depend upon the size of your final design. The sample box will use the dimensions and design presented in Fig. 3-68.

To minimize both cutting and assembling, the box employs a traditional butt joint. It is assembled with wood glue and finishing nails. The bottom of the box is cut to fit inside the walls. To assist you in your planning, Fig. 3-69 presents a standard butt joint assembly.

[1] Obtain sufficient lumber for the project. You can make the front and side panels from 1-×-4 stock. Recall that the actual width of a 1 × 4 is 3½ inches. The back piece for the project requires 1-×-12 pine. The actual width of a 1-×-12 board is 11¼ inches. Thus, the 1-×-12 board is the exact width of the back piece of the project. Note in Fig. 3-68 that the front panel of the box is 11¼ inches.

Although you will find that 1-×-12 material is expensive, a number of later projects also are made from this size stock. It can be difficult, at times, to find quality 12-inch-wide stock. The information in Chapter 1 on selecting pine can be very helpful.

[2] Measure and cut the front and two side panels to the lengths

Fig. 3-68. Design of the Candle Box.

suggested in Fig. 3-68. To simplify working with the 1-×-12 board, cut off a piece that is approximately 8 inches long. The back piece is 7 inches in length, so you will have a minimum of waste. By cutting a section off the board, both patterning and cutting are a great deal easier.

[3] Design and cut patterns for both the back piece and the front panel. Although you might want to duplicate the suggested design in Fig. 3-68, I encourage you to make your own designs. Remember to prepare the patterns to the actual dimensions of the piece they represent. After you have completed the pattern work, trace and cut the front panel and the back piece. A saber saw and a fine-toothed blade will work well for sawing the detail in both pieces.

[4] If you plan to hang the finished box, drill a ¼-inch-diameter hole in the upper center of the back piece. The hole is not necessary if you plan on placing the project on a flat surface.

[5] Measure and cut the two side panels to the suggested dimensions. If you prefer a wide box, simply increase the length of the two side panels. It will not affect the already prepared front and back pieces. You might find that a 3½-inch width is too small for your purposes. Simply increase the length of the side panels to arrive at a satisfactory width.

[6] Rout selected edges on the panels and back piece with a round-over bit and a table-mounted router. If a router is not available, sand the edges slightly rounded using 80-grit abrasive paper. Do not rout the inside bottom edges of the front and side panels.

[7] Using abrasive paper with grits from course to fine, sand all the surfaces and routed edges. Bring the various parts to finishing readiness.

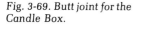
Fig. 3-69. Butt joint for the Candle Box.

[8] Assemble the two side panels to the back surface of the front panel. Use wood glue and finishing nails. Next, assemble the back piece to the oth-

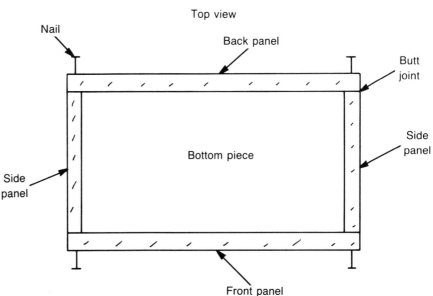

Top view

Nail

Back panel

Butt joint

Side panel

Bottom piece

Side panel

Front panel

er ends of the side panels. Be certain the joints fit tight. If they do not, clamp them with bar clamps until the glue is dry. Wipe off any excess glue from the surfaces.

[9] To prepare the bottom piece for the box, measure the inside dimensions of the box. Make the measurements at the bottom of the box. Cut a piece to these exact dimensions, slide the piece into the box, and nail from all four sides. It is not necessary to glue this piece in place.

For an alternative bottom, cut a piece to the exact outside dimensions of the bottom of the box. This will give you an added depth of ¾ inch inside the box. Glue and nail the piece to the bottom edges of the panels and also to the back piece. Rout its edges or sand them round.

PROJECT 21: NAPKIN HOLDER

A project that lends itself to both function and decoration is a Napkin Holder (Fig. 3-70). The design of this project is rather simple, but it is very effective in terms of both holding napkins in place and releasing them for use. The napkins lay on the base and a small board that slides up and down on dowels holds them in place. One or more napkins can be pulled out at a time. An added feature of the design is that the napkins do not need to be folded when placed in the holder. Figure 3-71 depicts the project design and its approximate dimensions.

The sliding piece on the project presents sufficient surface for tole painting a design. Although both the base and the sliding piece have their corners coved, you might want to have more scrollwork in your design. Also, to provide more surface for painting, you can easily widen the sliding piece. Modify the final design and dimensions of the project to meet your tastes and interests. The sample napkin holder, will use the dimensions presented in Fig. 3-71.

Fig. 3-70. Napkin Holder.

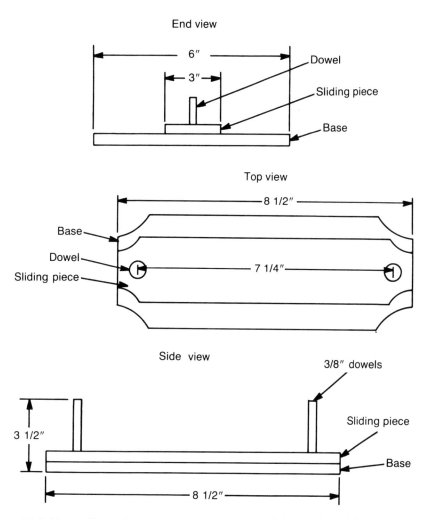

End view

6″

3″

Dowel

Sliding piece

Base

Top view

8 1/2″

Base

Dowel

Sliding piece

7 1/4″

Side view

3/8″ dowels

Sliding piece

3 1/2″

Base

8 1/2″

Fig. 3-71. Design of the Napkin Holder.

[1] You will need 1-×-8 pine for the base of the holder. If desired, you can increase the width of the base to 7¼ inches. Although the base then will take up a bit more counter or table space, it is not that significant. The larger width will eliminate the need to rip the stock to the suggested 6-inch width. Cut the base to the desired dimensions.

[2] You will make the sliding piece from 1-×4 pine or scrap material from wider stock. As suggested, you might want to increase its width to provide more area for tole painting. The length of this piece should be the same as for the base. Cut to the length and width you desire.

[3] You can cut the corners of both the base and the sliding piece by laying out the angle on one corner and cutting it off. Use the piece that is cut as a pattern for the remaining three corners. Simply align the straight edges of the cut piece with the corner edges, trace the angle, and cut. This procedure is a good technique for cutting corners to a uniform size and angle.

[4] Cut two pieces of ⅜-inch-diameter dowel to a length of 3½ inches.

These dowels are what the sliding piece moves up and down on to hold the napkins in place.

[5] Drill two ⅜-inch-diameter holes into the base to hold the dowels. The center of the dowels should be exactly 7¼ inches apart. Refer to Fig. 3-71 for the placement of the dowels. Drill the two holes to an approximate depth of ½ inch. Be certain both holes are the same depth.

[6] Next drill two ½-inch-diameter holes through the ends of the sliding piece. These holes also should be exactly 7¼ inches apart from their centers. The dowels need to fit through the two holes on the sliding piece for easy movement. The size of the holes make this possible. Make certain to place the sliding piece's holes in the center of the piece and to align them with one another. This is the surface that is exposed to view.

[7] You can round all of the edges of the various pieces with a round-over bit on a table-mounted router, or you can round the edges with abrasive paper. Round the ends of the dowels using abrasive paper. With this rounding procedure, the one end is easier to drive into the base hole and the other end looks more finished.

[8] Sand all surfaces and edges to a finishing readiness.

[9] Place wood glue on the walls of the two base holes. Drive the two dowels into the holes. Check that they stand erect. Allow the glue to dry. Place the sliding piece over the dowels and allow it to drop to the base surface.

PROJECT 22: SEWING BOARD

This Sewing Board (Fig. 3-72) is designed for those who need occasional access to needles, thread, and a sewing scissors. It holds these items and can be hung on the wall in a removed, but yet strategic location. It is a very functional unit, but one that also has some surface for tole painting. Although I generally make the Sewing Board from 1-×-8 pine, you can make it from 1-×-10 or 1-×-12 stock. The wider stock will provide for considerably more area for holding a range of threads and other possible accessories that you might want to hang on it. The length of the sample project will be 17 inches. Again, you can increase or decrease its length based on your own needs.

As you will note in Fig. 3-72, the project involves making three strips of wood that have ¼-inch-diameter dowels secured in them. The spools of thread fit over these dowels. An antique nail driven partially into the surface of the back board holds a pin cushion. A small wooden bracket attached to the surface of the board holds a sewing scissors in place. An additional dowel, with a larger diameter, also can be secured to the board to hold a thimble. Figure 3-73 presents two views of the project, along with some dimensions.

[1] Pattern and cut the back board from 1-×-8 stock. Use the dimensions in Fig. 3-73 for the sample project. Make a pattern of the top portion of the back board so its curved edges are uniform. If you prefer a more decorative edge on this portion of the board, pattern and cut the design using a saber saw and a fine cutting blade.

[2] Drill a hanging hole, using a ¼-inch-diameter bit or a countersink

116

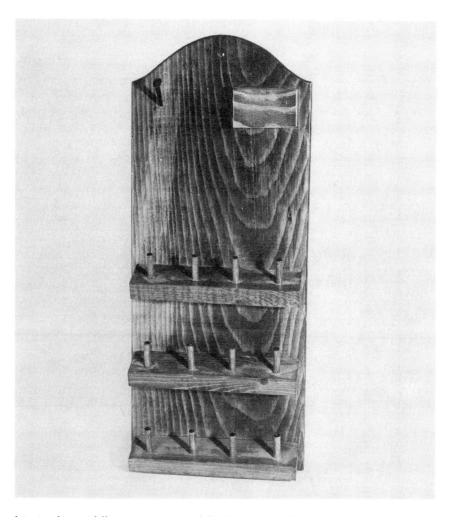

bit, in the middle, top section of the back board. You can hang the board on a large finishing nail, angled into the wall.

[3] Measure and cut three spool holders to a length of 6½ inches and a width of 1½ inches. You can make these pieces from scrap pieces of pine. If none is available, you can use 1-×-4 stock for the spool holders. As Fig. 3-73 indicates, cut the back edge of the spool holders at an angle. This angle permits the spools of thread to be placed onto the dowels more easily. It also enhances the overall appearance of the sewing board. Figure 3-74 presents, with dimensions, the area that you should cut from the back edges of the spool holders.

The easiest way to cut the strips to the desired angle is to use a band saw, its fence, and tilting table. You also can use a saber saw by setting the base at the desired angle. Most saber saws permit this type of angle cutting. You would be well advised to check the owner's manual on the proper procedures for making this type of cut with a saber saw.

117

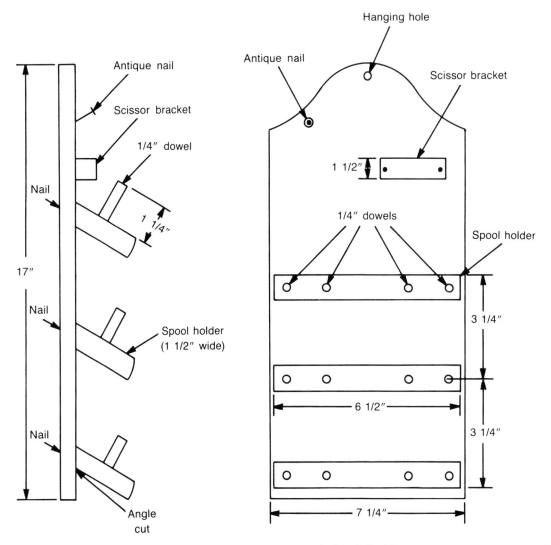

Side view

Front view

Hanging hole

Antique nail

Antique nail

Scissor bracket

Scissor bracket

1/4" dowel

1 1/2"

Nail

17"

1 1/4"

1/4" dowels

Spool holder

Nail

Spool holder
(1 1/2" wide)

3 1/4"

6 1/2"

Nail

3 1/4"

Angle
cut

7 1/4"

[4] Each spool holder must have four ¼-inch-diameter holes drilled into them for the ¼-inch-diameter dowels. The placement of the dowels should be approximately ½ inch from the front edge of the spool holder an equal distance apart and in line with one another. Measure, mark, and drill the four dowel holes in each of the spool holders. Drill the holes to a uniform depth of ¼ inch. Cut twelve ¼-inch-diameter dowels to a length of 1¼ inches. This length allows at least 1 inch to extend beyond the surface of the spool holder.

[5] Next prepare a bracket to hold the scissors. Refer to Fig. 3-73 for the placement of the bracket. Figure 3-75 presents the various parts of the bracket and its dimensions. Note that the front piece of the bracket is sawed to a thickness of ⅜ inch.

Fig. 3-73. Design of the Sewing Board.

Top view

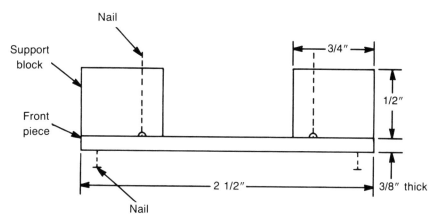

Top view

Fig. 3-74. Angle of the spool holder—side view.

The support blocks and the front piece of the bracket should be 1½ inches wide. The scissors are held between the two support blocks and the front piece. The area is sufficiently large to accommodate most standard sewing scissors.

[6] Rout the edges of the back board and the front edges of the spool holders. A round-over bit is best used on this project. Very little edge should be routed from the various parts. You can sand the outer edges of the front piece on the scissors bracket after you have secured it to the board.

[7] Using various grits of abrasive paper, sand all the surfaces and routed edges in preparation for the finishing process. Remove all dust before assembling.

[8] Attach the spool holders to the back board using glue and finishing nails. Drive the nails from the back surface of the back board into the holders. As indicated in Fig. 3-73, place the spool holders so that their bottom edges are at least 3¼ inches apart. This placement allows sufficient space between the bottom of the holders and the top of the dowels so that you can place and remove spools of thread with ease.

[9] Before you secure the spool holders to the board, glue and drive in place the ¼-inch-diameter dowels. Lightly round both ends of each dowel

Fig. 3-75. Scissors bracket.

Top

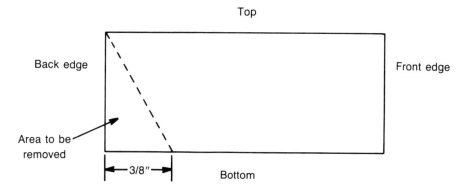

to help it penetrate into the drilled hole and make the exposed end more finished looking. Wipe off any excess glue.

[10] Measure and mark the locations of the holders on the board's surface. An effective procedure for securing the spool holders to the back board is to do them one at a time. It is best to begin with the bottom holder. Spread glue on the angled back edge and press in place on the board. Allow the glue to partially dry. Turn the board over and drive finishing nails into the spool holder while it is laying on a hard surface. Handle the assembly carefully so that the glued holder is not knocked out of place prior to nailing. Secure the remaining holders to the back board.

[11] Before you secure the scissors bracket, refer to Fig. 3-73 for its approximate location on the back board. You should place it high enough on the board so that the scissors will not hit the surface of the top spool holder when in place. You might want to have your scissors at hand during this procedure. Glue and nail the two support pieces of the bracket to the board's surface, placing them so that the front bracket piece will be flush with their outer edges. This makes the hole between them in which the scissors will fit. To secure the support pieces to the board, use wood glue and narrow wire nails. Usually, finishing nails will split them. You want these blocks well attached because they need to hold the scissors securely in place.

Using glue and small brads, nail the front piece of the bracket to the two support pieces. Refer to Fig. 3-73 for the relation between the support blocks and the front piece. Be certain to wipe off any excess glue that squeezes out during the assembling process.

[12] The final task is to drive a large antique nail, at an angle, opposite the scissors bracket, into the back board. You can purchase this type of square-head nail at most local hardware stores. It adds a nice touch for hanging a pin cushion on the sewing board.

PROJECT 23: SALT BOX WITH LID

The Salt Box with Lid (Fig. 3-76) represents another historic piece that was designed primarily for functional use. The box was originally designed to hold salt for household use. This function, of course, resulted in boxes of this design being historically called salt boxes. Although the box was no doubt made in a range of sizes, the actual dimensions were certainly based on household need. In addition to a diversity of sizes, most existing salt boxes from this Early American period are of a variety of shapes and designs. While some were clearly placed on a shelf or countertop, others have a drilled hole for hanging. It is also interesting to note how many of these early boxes were embellished with detailed carving or painting.

The project design represents a modification of a number of these original boxes. Its dimensions are partly dictated by the size of a standard 1 × 8. The design seeks to maximize material in order to minimize cost. Although the project box will hold standard 3-×-5-inch recipe cards, it also can be used for a variety of other storage functions. Its use is by no means limited to the kitchen. The design of the box is clearly decorative, and it can be enhanced

Fig. 3-76. Salt Box with Lid.

further via tole painting, woodburning, or carving. Its front and back board surface provide ample areas for a range of embellishments.

Figure 3-77 presents the box design and its dimensions. The lid with its knob is removable in this project. You can design the box with a hinged lid if desired. The knob is a standard hardwood knob that is available at most hardware stores or through various mail-order suppliers. You might prefer a fancier knob.

As indicated, you might prefer to modify the dimensions suggested in Fig. 3-77. Do some design work in relation to where you plan to place or hang the box. Also, design it to meet a particular storage need that you have. You also can modify the scroll design on the back board to conform more to your own tastes.

[1] The project can be made entirely from 1-×-8 stock. Combine the various dimensions presented in Fig. 3-77 to determine the actual amount of stock you will need. It is always best to select a board that is a bit longer than you actually need for a given project. The lid can be made from 1-×-6 stock if desired. Its width lends itself to this size board if you have a piece laying around.

121

Front view

Hanging hole

Knob

Lid

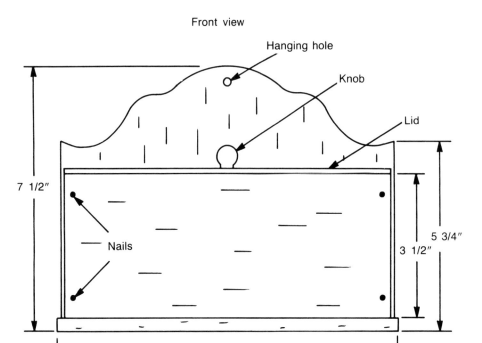

7 1/2"

5 3/4"

3 1/2"

Nails

7 1/4"

Side view

Knob

Lid

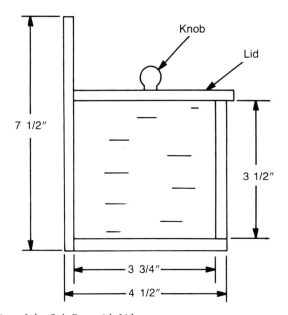

7 1/2"

3 1/2"

3 3/4"

4 1/2"

Fig. 3-77. Design of the Salt Box with Lid.

[2] Measure and cut both the back board and the bottom piece using the suggested dimensions. Decide how you want the scrollwork on the back board to look and make a pattern. This type of scrollwork should be patterned so that the two sides of the scroll match. After you have prepared the pattern, trace it on the surface of the back board and cut. A saber saw will do an excellent job in cutting the scrollwork.

[3] Drill a ¼-inch-diameter hanging hole in the upper center of the back board.

[4] Measure and cut the two side pieces of the box using the dimensions provided in Fig. 3-77. Lay out the sides and cut them with the grain. Be certain they are both the same length and width.

[5] Next, measure and cut the front piece of the box. It, too, should be cut with the grain. Refer to Fig. 3-77 for the dimensions for this part.

[6] Before you make the lid, you should rout the back board and bottom piece. Using a round-over bit, rout only the top edges of the scrollwork on the back board. Rout the front and side edges of the bottom board. You should rout the edges only slightly, especially on the bottom piece. After you have totally assembled the project, you can round the edges a bit more using abrasive paper. After assembly, you also can sand the edges that were not routed.

[7] Using a range of abrasive papers, sand all the surfaces to a finishing readiness. The next task is to assemble the box section to the back board and bottom piece, so you want to have everything properly sanded. Remove all sanding dust from the various parts.

[8] Using wood glue and small finishing nails, assemble the two side pieces to the front piece of the box. Be certain the edges are flush. Drive the nails from the front piece into the ends of the side pieces. Nail-punch the heads of the nails under the surface. Allow the assembly to dry.

[9] Glue and nail the back board to the bottom piece. Drive the finishing nails from the back surface of the back board into the edge of the bottom piece. Be certain the various edges are flush before nailing.

[10] Using wood glue and finishing nails, secure the box to the bottom piece and the back board. Drive the nails from the back surface of the back board, and from the bottom surface of the bottom piece. Use a nail punch to drive the heads of the finishing nails under the surface, especially on the bottom surface.

[11] Figure 3-78 presents the design of the lid, as well as its dimensions. Measure and cut the lid piece to the dimensions suggested.

[12] Rout the front and side edges of the lid. I use a cove bit on these three edges to enhance the overall appearance of the box and reduce the thick appearance of the lid. Use a table-mounted router for this procedure. Do not rout the back edge or the bottom edge. Only the top three edges should be routed.

[13] Using a range of abrasive papers, sand the routed edges and the lid's top surface to finishing readiness. Lightly sand all other edges, but do not round them with the abrasives.

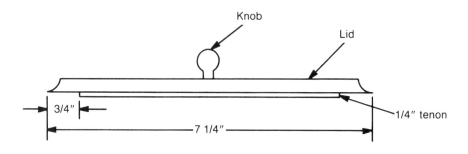

Front view

Knob

Lid

3/4"

7 1/4"

1/4" tenon

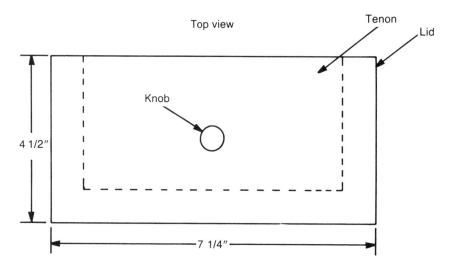

Top view

Tenon

Lid

Knob

4 1/2"

7 1/4"

[14] In order for the lid to remain in place on the box, you must make and attach a tenon to the bottom surface of the lid. Refer to Fig. 3-78 for information on the dimensions of the tenon. Cut the tenon from a piece of scrap material to a thickness of ¼ inch. Its length and width are a fraction smaller than the actual internal dimensions of the box. After the tenon is at-tached to the bottom surface of the lid, it must be able to fit neatly inside the box in order to hold the lid in place. Use a band saw to rip a scrap piece to the tenon thickness. You also can use a saber saw, but you must cut several strips to the appropriate dimensions, rather than one piece.

Using wood glue and small brads, secure the tenon to the bottom surface of the lid. Be certain the back edge of the tenon is flush with the back edge of the lid. Also, leave an equal distance on both sides of the tenon so that the lid will fit straight on the box. After you have secured the tenon to the lid, test for fit. You might need to sand some surface from the tenon edges in order to have a good fit.

Fig. 3-78. Salt Box lid.

[15] Using a ruler, locate the center of the lid and mark this point on its top surface. Place the lid knob at this location. If you are using a wooden knob with a screw, drill a small pilot hole for the screw through the lid. Then secure the knob to the lid with the screw. Another option is to glue the wooden knob to the lid's surface. If you are using glue, clamp the knob in place until the glue is dry.

PROJECT 24: FIVE BOARD STOOL

Although a Five-Board Stool (Fig. 3-79) is another historic design, its actual shape and size should be based on user need. The project can be made to function as a child's stool, a foot rest, a decorative piece or, if you are so inclined, a bench. The project also can be designed to be used as a standing stool. As a rule, these small stools can be somewhat hazardous if not used with care when standing on them. If you plan to use the project for a standing stool, you might want to increase the suggested dimensions to give the design more stability.

The stool design presented in Fig. 3-80 will serve as the project sample. You might want to modify the suggested dimensions to meet your own design needs. In addition to possible dimensional changes, you might want to change the leg design. Another design option is to pattern and cut a hand slot in the top board of the stool. You can cut the slot in the shape of a heart, if desired.

If you are inclined to tole painting, you might want to make the stool to a size that will accommodate a particular design. Spend some time working through both your functional needs and design preferences before you

Fig. 3-79. Five-Board Stool.

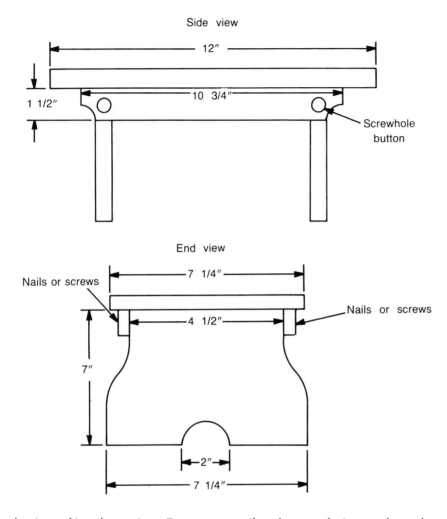

Side view

12"

10 3/4"

1 1/2"

Screwhole
button

End view

Nails or screws

7 1/4"

4 1/2"

Nails or screws

7"

2"

7 1/4"

begin crafting the project. Do some pencil and paper design work on the project.

Fig. 3-80. Design of the Five-Board Stool.

As noted in the project tasks, you can assemble the stool using either wood screws or finishing nails along with wood glue. Base your decisions on both your planned use and crafting preferences. If you are using wood screws, you will want to cover their heads using small wooden buttons. Although screws always make for a stronger project, they are not mandatory. The nature of the Five-Board Stool design places all the weight directly on the two legs.

[1] Use 1-×-8 stock for both the top piece and the legs. For the two side support pieces, you can use either scrap material or 1-×-4 stock. Since the support pieces are only 1½ inches wide, you can cut both pieces from a 12-inch length of 1 × 4.

[2] Measure and cut the top piece to the dimensions suggested in Fig. 3-80 or to those of your own design.

[3] Measure and cut the two legs to a length of 7 inches. As with the stool top, the standard 7¼ inch width of 1-×-8 material is also the actual width of the legs. The top portion of the legs that attach to the stool's top piece are, however, reduced to a width of 4½ inches. The edges of this reduced area must be flat and at least 1½ inches long in order to accommodate the support pieces. Refer to Fig. 3-80 to obtain an idea of these varying dimensions.

To ensure uniformity on the edges of the legs, I make a pattern. You also can measure and draw the curved areas on one leg and then cut the areas out with a saber saw. Use the finished leg as a pattern for the second leg.

You can pattern the round cutout area at the bottom of both legs using any round object with a 2-inch diameter. For example, a frozen orange juice can is effective. The cutout area is actually a partial circle that is traced and then cut from both legs. You can make the cuts easily with a saber saw. Prepare and cut the legs to conform with Fig. 3-80 or your own design.

[4] Measure and cut the two side support pieces to a length of 10¾ inches and a width of 1½ inches. To make the pieces more attractive, cut off the bottom corner on both ends of the two pieces. I make one rounded cut on one piece and then use it for a pattern for the other corners. Make the cuts with a saber saw.

[5] Using a table-mounted router and a round-over bit, rout the edges on both the top and bottom of the top piece. Only a portion of the edges of the legs should be routed. Do not rout the top or bottom edges, or the area where the side support pieces will be attached. Rout only the ends and the bottom edges of the side pieces that will be exposed. If you lack a router, use a small plane or abrasive paper to roll the various edges.

[6] Sand the routed edges and all surfaces using a range of abrasive grits. The surfaces need to be prepared for finishing. Remove all the sanding dust prior to assembly.

[7] Prior to beginning the assembly process, refer to Fig. 3-80 to determine where the side support pieces are attached to the legs. Using wood glue and finishing nails, secure one side piece to both legs. Be certain the top edge of the side piece is flush with the top edge of the legs. Also, be certain the legs are straight up and down when you nail the side pieces in place. Repeat the procedure with the second side piece. After both side pieces are secured to the legs, the assembly should be stable; it should not rock.

[8] Spread wood glue on the top surface of the legs and on the top edge of both side pieces. Center the stool top on the leg assembly and nail in place. It is best to nail into the legs and the support pieces. Along with the wood glue, the nails will give you a more stable stool.

[9] Using a nail punch, drive the heads of the finishing nails under the surface of the boards.

PROJECT 25: TISSUE HOLDER

The Tissue Holder (Fig. 3-81) is another functional piece that lends itself to a range of decorative embellishment. The holder presents sufficient surface for tole painting, stenciling, woodburning, or even carving. The project is de-

Fig. 3-81. Tissue Holder.

signed to accommodate a standard 4½-inch-square box of tissue that is approximately 5¼ inches tall. This size holder is ideal because it occupies a minimum of space wherever placed. The holder is designed to slip over the tissue box. There is no need to have a bottom on the holder. The tissues are removed through the oval cut in the top piece of the holder.

If you use the more standard size of tissue box, you can modify the project easily. The dimensions for a standard box of tissues are usually about 10 inches long, 4¾ inches wide, and from 3 to 4 inches high. For this type of tissue box, increase the length of the oval the top piece. You would be well advised to check the dimensions of the box of tissues that you normally use prior to making the holder. As a rule, I make holders at least ¼ inch larger on all the dimensions of the actual box of tissues. This extra size ensures that the holder can be easily placed over or removed from the tissue box.

Figure 3-82 presents the side walls of the project, along with their dimensions. A top view is also provided to assist you in assembling the walls. The top view of the walls and the dimensions are presented in Fig. 3-83. Note that the walls are assembled using a standard butt joint.

[1] Measure and cut the side walls using standard 1-×-6 stock. The width of 1-×-6 stock is 5½ inches. Since the grain of the wood should run lengthwise on the walls of the box, this is the exact width needed. You need only to

Side view: wall 1 (2 panels)

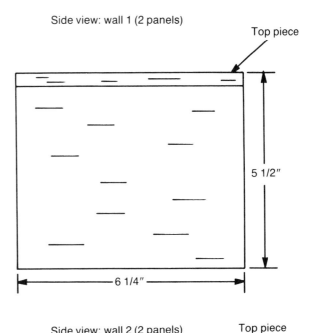

Top piece

5 1/2"

6 1/4"

Side view: wall 2 (2 panels)

Top piece

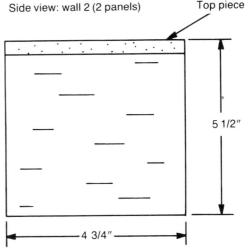

5 1/2"

4 3/4"

Fig. 3-82. Side view of the Tissue Holder.

cut the walls to length as indicated in Fig. 3-82. This 5½-inch width will give a ¼-inch clearance between the top of the tissue box and the bottom surface of the holder top.

[2] The wall edges are not routed on this design. After you have totally assembled the project, use abrasive to lightly round those edges that are exposed.

[3] Sand all the surfaces of the walls to finishing readiness. Remove all sanding dust.

[4] Using wood glue and finishing nails, assemble the walls. Refer to Fig. 3-83 to note how the walls are assembled. Be certain the edges of the

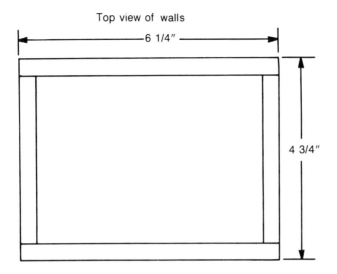

Top view of walls

|← 6 1/4" →|

4 3/4"

various walls are all flush with one another. Wipe off any excess glue that squeezes out during assembly.

[5] The top piece of the holder should be 6¼ inches square, assuming that you have cut the walls to the appropriate dimensions. Figure 3-86 presents the top piece, along with the cutout area and dimensions. You will need a

Fig. 3-83. Top view and butt joints of the Tissue Holder.

Fig. 3-84. Top piece of the Tissue Holder.

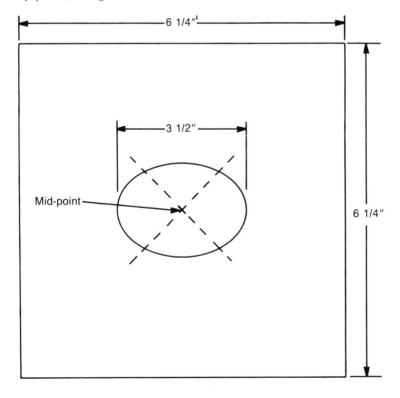

|← 6 1/4" →|

← 3 1/2" →

Mid-point

6 1/4"

piece of 1-×-8 stock to make the top section of the holder. Measure and cut the top piece.

[6] An effective way to pattern the 3½-inch-long oval in the top section is to use the top of an actual tissue box. Simply tear the top portion of the box off and use it as your pattern. Be certain to measure and find the midpoint of the top piece and place the pattern accordingly. You might find that the actual length of the box oval varies from the suggested 3½-inch length. Whatever its dimension, it is acceptable.

You can cut out the oval area using a saber saw. Drill a hole through the oval into which the blade of the saber saw can be inserted. Neatly cut along the patterned line. You will want to support the piece during the cutting function.

[7] To give the holder a more finished appearance, rout the top edges of the top piece and also the edges of the oval. A table-mounted router with a round-over bit is effective for this procedure.

[8] Using wood glue and finishing nails, secure the top piece to the wall assembly. Using a nail punch, drive the heads of all finishing nails under the surface of the boards.

[9] Finish sanding the routed edges and the top surface of the holder. Also, lightly round all the exposed edges of the wall assembly using abrasive paper.

PROJECT 26: WINE RACK

This project is primarily functional, but it does provide some surface for embellishment. Wine racks are relatively easy to make even if you have limited woodworking experience. The primary issue with the project has to do with how many bottles you want the rack to hold. To teach you how to make a wine rack, this project has been designed to hold six wine bottles (Fig. 3-85). Once you understand the basic procedures in making this design, you can increase or decrease the size of the rack to meet your own needs.

In order for the wine bottles to rest evenly in the rack, it is necessary to vary the size of the holders on the front and back sections. The back portion of the rack has holders of larger diameter because they must accommodate the base section of the bottle. Correspondingly, the front holders are smaller because they hold the necks of the bottles. It is worth noting that there is wide variability among wine bottles both in length and diameter. You might find that a particular brand needs a specially designed rack. Using the various procedures for this project, you can custom-make a rack. Figure 3-86 presents the Wine Rack project and some of its dimensions.

The project is designed to stand on a counter or bar area. You might prefer to secure small eye screws to the top frame and hang the rack. Strong but decorative chain is available in most hardware stores for hanging items. This is an effective way to save counter or bar space but still have easy access to the rack and its contents. If you will hang the rack, be certain that it is well assembled. Figure 3-87 presents a side view of the rack, with dimensions.

Fig. 3-85. Wine Rack.

[1] The rack is best made from 1-×-6 stock. The curved areas that hold the wine bottles are half circles that result after the 1-×-6 stock has been cut into two pieces. Measure and cut two 1-×-6 boards that are 14 inches long.

[2] This task requires the use of a circle cutter and a drill press. There are a number of options to using the circle cutter. You can cut circles of the appropriate diameter using a saber saw. You can drill the smaller circles with a different type of circle cutter that can be used in an electric drill. Another option is to saw the two boards in half and then cut out the partial circles using a saber saw. However you proceed, careful measurement is critical. Refer to Fig. 3-86 and the suggested dimensions as you begin.

One board will serve as the front portion of the rack and will have three holes with diameters of 1½ inches. The second board is the back section and will have three holes that are 3½ inches in diameter. Prior to cutting the holes, mark their exact location on the boards. Figure 3-88 presents the layout of both boards, as well as the appropriate dimensions. Measure and mark the two 1-×-6 boards using the suggested dimensions.

Set the circle cutter to make a 3½-inch-diameter hole. Remember that the cutter is set at the radius of the circle. In this instance, set the cutter at 1¾ inches. It is best to clamp the board to the drill press table when you

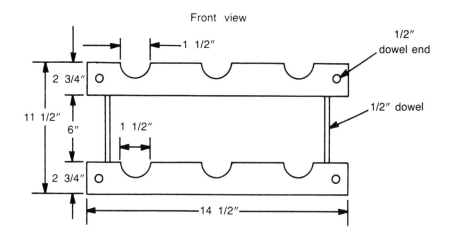

Front view

1 1/2"

1/2" dowel end

2 3/4"

1/2" dowel

11 1/2"

6"

1 1/2"

2 3/4"

14 1/2"

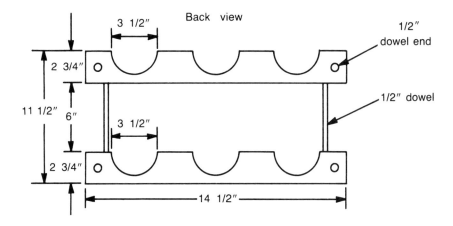

Back view

3 1/2"

1/2" dowel end

2 3/4"

1/2" dowel

11 1/2"

6"

3 1/2"

2 3/4"

14 1/2"

Fig. 3-86. Front and back view of the Wine Rack.

Fig. 3-87. Side View of the Wine Rack.

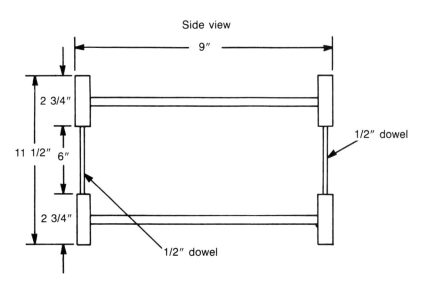

Side view

9"

2 3/4"

1/2" dowel

11 1/2"   6"

2 3/4"

1/2" dowel

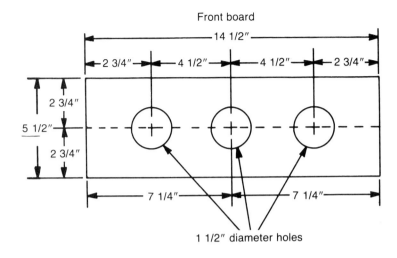

Front board

14 1/2"

2 3/4" — 4 1/2" — 4 1/2" — 2 3/4"

2 3/4"

5 1/2"

2 3/4"

7 1/4" — 7 1/4"

1 1/2" diameter holes

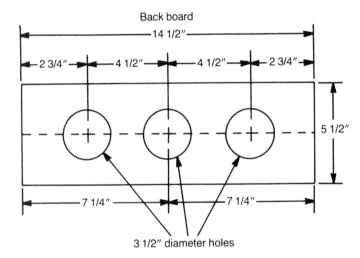

Back board

14 1/2"

2 3/4" — 4 1/2" — 4 1/2" — 2 3/4"

5 1/2"

7 1/4" — 7 1/4"

3 1/2" diameter holes

are cutting the holes. The cutters are capable of pulling the board from your hand and causing injury. Use good judgment and safety precautions. Clamp the board when you are cutting all the holes. Cut the three 3½-inch-diameter holes in the back board.

Reset the circle cutter to ¾ inch to make the 1½-inch-diameter holes in the front board. Clamp the board and cut the three holes.

[3] Although a band saw is the most effective tool to cut the boards into two sections, you can use a saber saw. Saw both the front board and the back board into two equal sections. The center of the 1-×-6 board is 2¾ inches, and this point should already be marked from laying out the circles. Refer to Fig. 3-86 to note how the boards will look after they have been sawed.

[4] Assemble the rack and secure it using ½-inch-diameter dowels. Cut four dowels to a length of 9 inches. Next, cut four dowels to a length of 6 inches. Use the shorter dowels to reassemble the front and back boards (Fig.

Fig. 3-88. Front and back hole areas of the Wine Rack.

134

3-86). Use the 9-inch-long dowels to tie the two sections together (Fig. 3-87). Lightly sand the edges of each dowel on their ends. This slight rounding makes it easier to drive the dowels into their drilled holes.

[5] You need to drill ½-inch-diameter holes through the front and back boards to accommodate the 9-inch-long dowels. The dowels penetrate through the boards and are exposed on the outer surfaces. This makes for a more attractive and stronger rack. Note the dowel ends marked on Fig. 3-86. Measure and mark on the two front pieces where the ½-inch holes should be drilled. Be certain they are placed in the approximate center of the boards near the ends. Do not place the holes too close to the end of the boards or they will split when the dowels are driven into the holes.

To ensure that the dowel holes are in alignment, it is best to drill through both a front and back section at the same time. Stack a front piece on top of a back piece and drill the ½-inch-diameter hole through both pieces. Hold the two pieces tightly together during the drilling function. Repeat the process on the other end of the stack, and with the other front and back section. Do not assemble the rack. Some additional tasks remain.

[6] To accommodate the 6-inch-long dowels, you must drill holes into the edges of both the front and back pieces. Refer to Fig. 3-86 for the location of these dowels. The drilled holes need to be ½ inch in diameter and ½ inch in depth. Measure and mark the location of the holes on all the pieces. Be sure they are centered and not too close to the edge. Set the stop on your drill press so that all the holes are drilled to an equal depth. If you are using an electric drill, wrap a piece of tape around the bit at the ½-inch point. The tape will serve as an effective guide in determining depth. Carefully drill all the holes.

[7] Although you might want to rout the various edges, I find that going over them with abrasive paper is equally effective. Remove the sharpness of the edges with the abrasives.

[8] Sand all surfaces to finishing readiness.

[9] It is best to assemble the front and back sections first and then join the two assemblies with the 9-inch dowels. Spread a tad of wood glue along the walls of the ½-inch holes and drive the 6-inch dowels in place. Be certain to tap the dowels to the bottom of the drilled holes. After the front and back assemblies are together, glue and dowel the two sections together using the 9-inch-long dowels. Again, spread glue on the walls of the holes and then drive in the dowels. The ends of the dowels should be flush with the outer surfaces when in place. Allow the glue to dry. Sand the ends of the dowels after the glue has dried so that they are clean and flush with the various surfaces.

PROJECT 27: FIREPLACE MATCH BOX

Although one of the functions of the Fireplace Match Box (Fig. 3-89) is indicated in its name, there are numerous other uses for the box. For example, the box can be used to hold drinking straws. Another obvious function is to hold pencils while placed on a desk. No doubt, with some reflection, you

Fig. 3-89. Fireplace Match Box.

can devise even more uses for this neat little box. An added feature of the box is that it can be either placed on a surface or hung on a nail.

Unlike most traditional match boxes that are placed by a fireplace, this one is quite small. It will hold a cluster of the large fireplace matches, but it does not occupy a great deal of space. I think it is more attractive and somewhat more tastefully done than the usual large boxes. In part, both the size and the design of this box have to do with the kind of material that is used.

This project is made from ⅜-inch thick batting, which is usually 2⅜ inches wide. Although it is somewhat more expensive than standard pine boards, batting is a material that you should become familiar with for crafting. Most lumberyards stock batting, and often it is stacked with trim material. You also can make the match box from standard pine, but I hope you at least explore the use of this excellent material for crafting. Incidentally, as with trim, batting is usually totally free of knots and other niceties that you find in No. 3 Common pine.

Figure 3-90 depicts the match box and also its various dimensions. The bottom section of the box is cut to the internal dimensions of the box and is secured inside. You might want to modify some of the design or scrollwork to conform more to your own tastes. The box offers sufficient surface on both the front and back panels for a tole-painted design.

[1] You will need at least 4 feet of 2⅜-inch-wide batting that is ⅜ inch thick. This length will be more than enough to build the box. You will find that you frequently must buy batting in rather sizable lengths. I think you will find that you will develop projects of your own using this material.

Because all of the panels have some type of scroll cut on them, it is best to cut each at least ½ inch longer than required. Although this procedure is somewhat wasteful of wood, it greatly simplifies both the patterning and cutting tasks. Cut the four panels to the lengths suggested in Fig. 3-90. Remember to add ½ inch to each length. You will measure and cut the bottom section after you assemble the box.

[2] Patterns are critical to this design, especially if you plan to have scrollwork similar to that shown in Fig. 3-89. You will need separate patterns for both the back and front panels. You can design the side panel directly onto the surface of the wood. Use the dimensions suggested in Fig. 3-90 and then draw a curved line joining the two points. Cut out one side panel and then use it for the pattern for the second panel. Use a saber saw for cutting.

Using construction paper, design and cut your patterns for the front and back panels. A good pattern procedure is to measure and cut the paper to the width of the panels. You do not need to make the pattern the full length of the panel. Fold the paper in half and pencil on your scroll design on one side. Using scissors, cut along the penciled line while the paper is folded. Open the paper and you should have two perfectly matched sides.

Trace the pattern designs onto the respective panels and cut them out using a saber saw and a fine-toothed blade. Take your time when you are making the cuts. You will notice that this thinner wood cuts both more easily

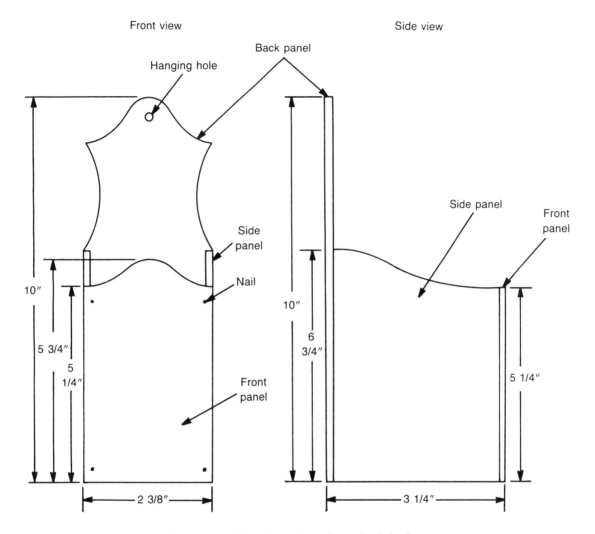

Front view

Side view

Back panel

Hanging hole

Side panel

Nail

Side panel

Front panel

10"

5 3/4"

5 1/4"

Front panel

10"

6 3/4"

5 1/4"

2 3/8"

3 1/4"

Fig. 3-90. Design of the Fireplace Match Box.

and more quickly than pine of standard thickness.

[3] I do not rout the edges on this project because the batting is too thin. It can be done but I prefer to simply use abrasive paper.

[4] If you plan to hang the box, drill a hole in the upper center of the back panel. Then sand all the surfaces to finishing readiness. You can sand the edges after you assemble the box.

[5] For assembling the box, it is best to use small wire brads that are at least ⅝ inch long. These, along with wood glue, make for a well-assembled project. Secure the front panel to the two side panels first. Spread a bead of glue on the edges of the side panels and nail the front panel to them. Wipe off any excess glue. After spreading glue on the back edges of the side panels, nail the back panel to them. Place the brads strategically to ensure a strong assembly. If you have a fine-pointed nail punch, tap the heads of the brads under the wood's surface. Allow the glue to dry.

[6] Measure the internal dimensions of the bottom of the box and prepare the bottom piece. Spread some wood glue on the inside walls and slide the bottom piece in place. It should fit flush with the bottom edges of the panels. Secure it in place with a series of brads on all sides. Allow the glue to dry.

[7] Using abrasive paper, slightly roll all the edges on the box. You might want to sand the surface of the bottom piece along with the bottom edges of the panels. Prepare the surface for finishing.

PROJECT 28: DECORATIVE CANDLE HOLDER

This project is a decorative and functional piece that is turned on the wood lathe (Fig. 3-91). If you have a wood lathe, no doubt you are already aware of the range of project possibilities that this tool presents.

Without exception, the wood lathe is the most versatile and enjoyable of the large woodworking tools. It is ideally suited to the hobbyist woodworker. The lathe not only provides a vehicle for relaxation and endless satisfaction, it also can produce an array of both functional and decorative pieces. If you do not have a lathe, I hope this project sufficiently peaks your interest that you consider purchasing one. Although a somewhat costly tool, lathes are often available used. Before you buy one, be certain to discuss lathes with someone who is familiar with their use and the quality of those available.

Fig. 3-91. Decorative Candle Holders.

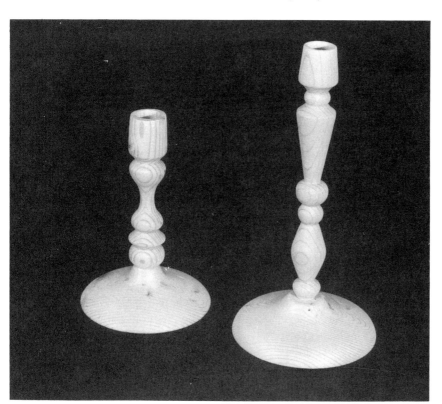

138

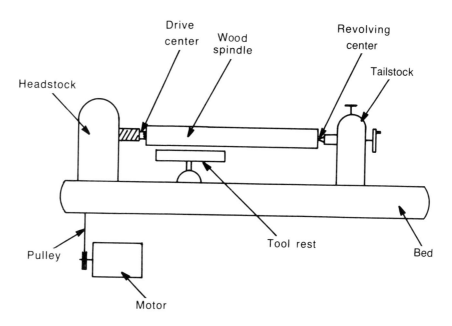

Headstock

Drive center

Wood spindle

Revolving center

Tailstock

Pulley

Tool rest

Bed

Motor

Fig. 3-92. Spindle turning.

This dictum also applies to turning tools and the range of accessories available for wood lathes.

There are two basic ways of turning wood on a lathe. The first, and certainly the most popular, method is what is generally called *spindle turning*. Spindle turning is accomplished by using both gouges and chisels while a spindle of wood is held between the centers. Figure 3-97 presents the basic parts of a lathe with a spindle of wood in place for turning.

Spindle turning also can be done with scrapers. Figure 3-93 pictures a selection of turning tools including gouges, chisels, scrapers, and a parting tool. A number of books are available to assist you in learning how to use and sharpen the various turning tools. In many communities, wood-turning classes are also available.

The second basic way to turn wood on a lathe is what is called *faceplate turning*. As the name implies, a faceplate is secured to the round block of wood. The faceplate is then threaded on the headstock spindle. For faceplate turning, you can use either scrapers or different sizes of bowl gouges. The use of bowl gouges requires some skill to effectively make them work. You might, initially, want to use scrapers for making projects while doing faceplate turning. Scrapers do not generally leave the surface of the wood as smooth or finished as do gouges and chisels. You can remedy this problem easily, however, by using various grits of abrasive papers.

A Decorative Candle Holder is an enjoyable and functional project to turn on the lathe. Depending upon your own preference, you can turn candle holders between centers, or you can use the faceplate method. The Decorative Candle Holder project is turned using a 3-inch faceplate. This does not, however, preclude using the spindle method for making the holders.

You will find that pine is a fun and challenging wood to turn, whether

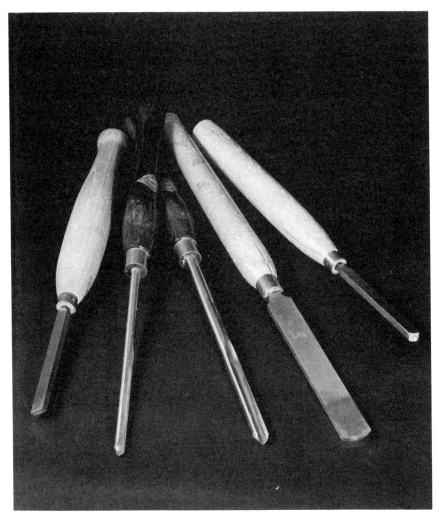

you use scrapers or cutting tools. Pine is also an excellent and inexpensive
wood to use to further develop your turning skills. Although most turners prefer
working with the various hardwoods, any number of production wood turners
work almost exclusively with pine.

This project is best turned from 2-inch stock. I use 2-×-6 material for the
base of the Decorative Candle Holder and a piece of 2-×-4 stock for the holder
spindle. It is generally less expensive to purchase material in standard lengths.

Before you begin this project, you might want to do some design work.
You can design the spindle portion of the holder to any length. Then increase
or decrease the diameter of the base in relation to this length. Figure 3-94
presents the sample project, with its dimensions.

[1] Using a band saw or saber saw, cut a 5½-inch-diameter round block
from a piece of 2 × 6. You can pattern the circle using a school compass

Fig. 3-93. Turning tools.

or similar device. This block will be the base of the candle holder.

[2] Saw a length of 2 × 4 that is 1½ inches square and 8 inches long. Recall that a standard 2 × 4 is 1½ inches thick. This piece will become the spindle of the candle holder. Be certain the ends of the piece are both square.

[3] Spread wood glue on one end of the 8-inch piece and also on the center surface of the 5½-inch-round block. Using a bar clamp, clamp the assembly together. When clamping, be careful that the spindle does not slide off-center on the glue. The spindle needs to be centered on the base block or it will turn off-center when you place it on the lathe. While the assembly is under pressure from the clamp, allow the glue to dry.

[4] Attach a 3-inch faceplate to the bottom surface of the 5½-inch-round block. Be sure to center the faceplate on the block. Use wood screws that are sufficiently long so that the assembly does not pull away from them during the turning process. Mount the assembly and faceplate on the headstock spindle.

Fig. 3-94. Candle Holder.

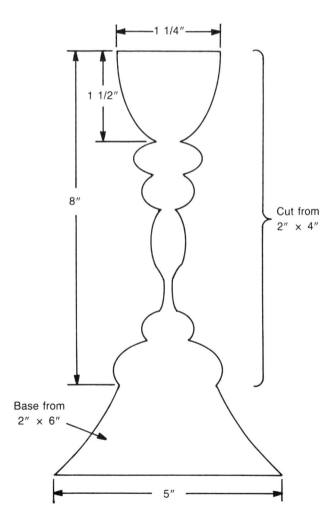

141

[5] After the assembly is secured to the headstock, it is a good practice to place a pointed revolving center in the tailstock and bring it forward into the spindle. This setup will not only make the assembly more stable for turning, but will also prevent it from tearing away from the faceplate screws. Figure 3-95 presents this lathe setup. The revolving center in the tailstock also will mark the exact center of the candle cup of the holder, greatly simplifying the drilling of the hole in the candle base.

[6] Depending upon whether you plan to use gouges or scrapers, align the tool rest accordingly. If you are using scrapers, place the tool rest slightly above the centerline of the assembly. If you are using gouges, place the tool rest below the centerline.

Effective scrapers for this type of project are a 1- and ½-inch round nose. If needed, you can use a ½-inch square nose chisel as a scraper. Generally this tool is used for cutting; however occasionally it is an effective scraper. A parting tool also can be helpful. If you prefer the cutting method, use a ⅜-inch spindle gouge, a 1-inch skew chisel, and a 1¼-inch roughing-out gouge. For shaping the base, you might want to use a ½-inch spindle gouge.

[7] Begin turning by roughing out the spindle and base to roundness. It is imperative that both be trued prior to any decorative turning. Prior to shaping the base and making decorative forms in the spindle, decide how you want the final candle holder to appear. You might want to refer to Fig. 3-91 or Fig. 3-92 for a few ideas. It is always best to have a general idea of the final shape of a piece before you begin to turn.

In order to have sufficient wood to hold the base of a candle, leave the cup end of the holder with at least a 1¼-inch diameter. It also should be approximately 1½ inches long. The base of a candle is usually about ¹³⁄₁₆ inch in diameter. Plan your turning accordingly.

[8] After you have turned the base and spindle, use a range of abrasive grits on the wood's surface. On pine, 100-grit sandpaper is sufficiently coarse to begin sanding the surface. I generally finish sanding with a 220-grit abrasive. Bring the entire surface to finishing readiness.

[9] Remove the assembly from the lathe and unscrew the faceplate. You will need to drill the candle base's hole in the cup area of the spindle. As

Fig. 3-95. Assembly on lathe: faceplate.

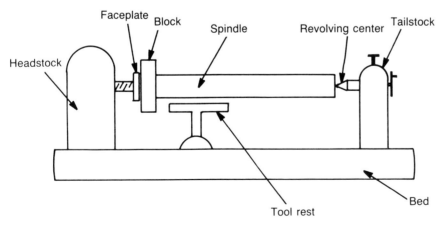

indicated, most candles have a $^{13}/_{16}$-inch base. Unfortunately, this is not always true. You might want to drill the hole to a diameter compatible with the candle you plan to use in the holder. A ¾-inch-diameter hole will accommodate many types of candles.

Drill the candle cup's hole using a drill press. I use a forstner style $^{13}/_{16}$-inch bit. Use the indentation made by the revolving center as the point of entry for the drill bit. Take your time with the drilling function so you do not ruin the candle holder.

[10] Use wood filler to plug the screw holes in the base of the holder.

[11] Sand the entire surface to a finishing readiness.

PROJECT 29: ANNUAL CHRISTMAS CANDLE HOLDER

This project, although seasonal, is one of those small items that is great fun to design and craft. (See Fig. 3-96.) I have noted how popular small items with the year on them are with individuals. Dated Christmas items seem especially popular. I began making this project in the early seventies and, each year, individuals look forward to obtaining the new holder for the year.

The interesting part of this project is that the basic design does not change significantly from year to year. The dimensions, including the Christmas tree, remain essentially the same. You do, however, need to design the numbers for each new year. As you will discover, some years are more difficult to design than others. Fortunately, the first letter is fixed, at least for a few years. The 1987 candle holder is a relatively easy sequence to design and cut. The eight can be patterned using a school compass, and the seven can be drawn freehand.

Fig. 3-96. 1987 Candle Holder.

I use a $^{7}/_{16}$-inch-diameter angel chime candle for the project. It is best

to drill the candle hole in the top edge of the second number to give the holder a more balanced appearance.

You will find that other objects can be integrated into a candle holder. For example, you can use a bear in place of the Christmas tree. You also can use other items, symbolic of some event. This type of project presents you with a range of design possibilities.

You can make the holder easily from scrap pieces of 1-×-4 stock. Figure 3-97 presents the outline of the project, along with suggested dimensions. The project is designed to be easily accommodated on a piece of 1-×-4 stock, thus keeping material costs to a minimum.

[1] Measure and cut a piece of 1 × 4 to a length of at least 7 inches. This length provides ample material for both patterning and cutting.

[2] Design and make a pattern from construction paper. Although you can draw the entire holder freehand onto the wood, a pattern makes the process much easier. Refer to Fig. 3-97 for the various dimensions. You might, of course, want to vary them or even alter the design.

Trace the pattern onto the 7-inch piece of wood and cut using either a saber saw or floor-model scroll saw. If you use a saber saw, take your time when making the various cuts, especially around the tree branches. Forcing the saw blade to make a sharp cut can result in a broken project. Plan your cuts—how they will begin and where they will end.

[3] If you are using small angel chime candles, drill a 7/16-inch-diameter hole in the top center of the second number. Drill the hole to a depth of no more than 3/8 inch. If the top portion of the number is rather narrow, adjust the hole depth accordingly. When you drill, be sure to support that portion of the number where the hole is to be made. The pressure of the bit could break the number.

[4] Sand the surfaces and edges in preparation for finishing.

Fig. 3-97. Design of the 1987 Candle Holder.

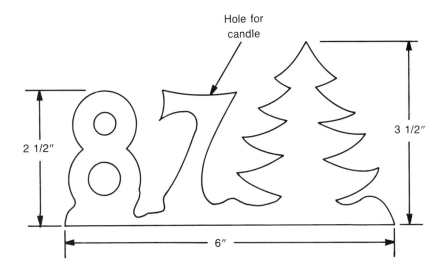

Hole for candle

2 1/2"

3 1/2"

6"

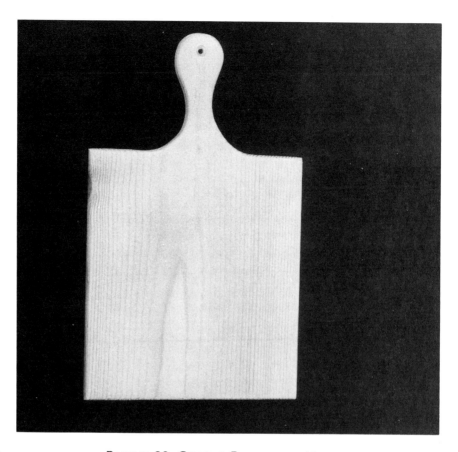

Fig. 3-98. Cutting Board
with Handle.

PROJECT 30: CUTTING BOARD WITH HANDLE

This project is a basic design that can be both functional and decorative. If you want a cutting board to provide a range of functions, Fig. 3-98 shows the design to use. Best of all, this design can be made to dimensions that will meet very specific needs. You can design it as a bread cutting board or, if desired, you can craft a smaller unit for cutting cheese. Although pine does not have the durability of hard maple, cutting boards made from pine will last many years.

In addition to a range of functions, the project also provides considerable surface for tole painting or stenciling. You also can modify the project both in size and shape. You might, for example, have a tole design that requires a larger board than the suggested project. Simply increase the overall dimensions to meet your specific need.

The project is relatively simple to draw freehand on the board's surface. Although you can make a pattern for the handle, it is not mandatory. You can measure and mark the approximate midpoint of the board and then use the bottom edge of a coffee can to pattern the curved handle areas. You can vary the width and length of the handle to meet your design needs. I drill a hole in the handle for hanging the board. If desired, you can thread a leath-

145

er boot string through the hole for hanging. Figure 3-99 presents the board's design, with some approximate dimensions.

[1] As shown in Fig. 3-99, you can use 1-×-8 stock for the project. The actual width of a 1 × 8 is 7¼ inches, so you only need to cut the board to length. In order to simplify patterning and cutting the board's handle, it is best to cut the board at least ½ inch longer than needed. Thus, cut the 1-×-8 board to a length of at least 12½ inches.

[2] Before you pattern the curved areas of the handle, measure and mark the center of the board. Draw a light line marking the center, through the handle area. This line serves as an effective guide for patterning the handle.

[3] Either draw the handle freehand or use a coffee can to make the

Fig. 3-99. Design of the Cutting Board with Handle.

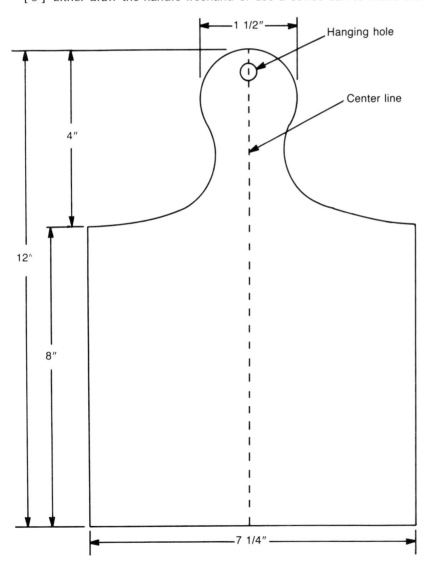

146

curves. The important thing is that the handle and its curved areas are the same on both sides. Cut out the handle area using a saber saw.

[4] Drill a ¼-inch-diameter hole in the upper center portion of the handle.

[5] Rout the edges on both sides of the board. A round-over bit and table-mounted router is best for this function. You might prefer to roll the edges using abrasive paper and a small hand plane.

[6] Using a range of abrasive grits, sand both surfaces and also the edges of the board. You want a good, smooth surface for finishing. As discussed in Chapter 4, remember to use a nontoxic oil of the board is to be used with food.

PROJECT 31: KEY HOLDER

The Key Holder is primarily a functional project (Fig. 3-100). It can, however, be enhanced with a variety of procedures to make it more decorative. There is no reason why pieces that are primarily functional cannot be embellished. For example, although a Key Holder might be placed in the basement stairway or the garage, it does not mean that it cannot be attractive.

The design of the project is simple but, with small pegs or dowels, it becomes a rather delightful piece. Although you might prefer something a bit more elaborate, you can make this project from 1-×-4 stock. If you prefer a wider board or more scrollwork, you might want to use a 1-×-6 board, or even a 1-×-8 piece. If you are interested in tole painting or some fancy wood-burning, you might want to consider the wider wood.

Rather than buying commercial pegs for the project, you might want to use ⅛-inch-diameter dowels. Using dowels keeps the cost of the project down, but does not greatly distract from the project. You can cut the pegs to any desired length and place them in drilled holes on the board. Although I have

Fig. 3-100. Key Holder. limited the number of pegs used on the sample project, you might want to

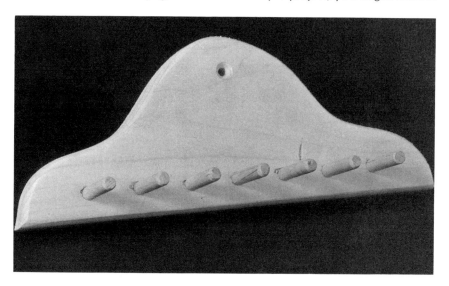

increase or decrease their number. This, again, is one of those planning issues that you must address in your design work.

If you prefer something other than dowels or commercial pegs, consider using small brass cup hangers. These small devices have a threaded end that can be screwed directly into the board. The bent front portion of the holder serves to hold the individual key or a set on a chain. You need chains to hang keys on dowels or pegs. Cup hangers eliminate the need for chains.

Figure 3-101 presents an outline of the project, as well as some approximate dimensions. You might want to change the design or its dimensions significantly to meet a particular need. The various tasks would be the same regardless of size or shape.

[1] As indicated, the project uses 1-×-4 stock. Measure and cut a piece to a length of 9½ inches. Although the sample project is 9 inches long, the additional ½ inch makes both patterning and cutting easier.

[2] Using construction paper, make a pattern of the holder. You might prefer to do some measuring and then draw the upper scroll area freehand. In whatever way you design the holder, be certain the curves are the same on both sides. Using a saber saw, cut the holder to its final shape.

[3] Measure and mark the location of the pegs or dowels. As Fig. 3-101 suggests, I tend to leave about 1 inch between each peg. You might want to reduce this dimension in order to place more pegs on the board. The pegs should be at least ½ inch from the bottom edge of the holder. In addition to the location of the pegs, you should measure and mark for the hanging hole.

[4] If you are using ⅛-inch-diameter dowels for the pegs, drill holes this diameter at the marked locations. Drill the holes to a uniform depth of at least ⅜ inch to ensure that the pegs all extend out from the board the same distance. Drill a ¼-inch-diameter hanging hole at the marked location.

[5] Cut the dowels to a length of at least 1¼ inches. Using sandpaper, round the cut edges on both ends of each dowel. Rounding the dowels makes driving them into their drilled holes much easier. It also makes the outer end

Fig. 3-101. Design of the Key Holder.

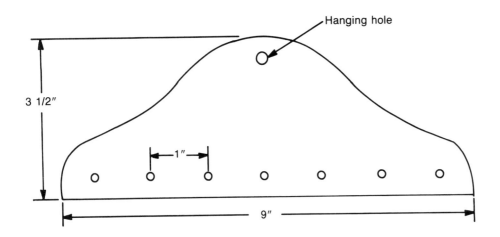
Hanging hole

3 1/2"

1"

9"

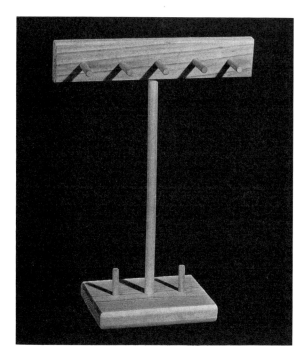

Fig. 3-102. Standing
Necklace and Ring Holder.

of each dowel look more finished. Do not place the dowels into the board until you have completed the following tasks.

[6] Round the edges of the holder using either a table-mounted router or abrasive paper.

[7] Sand the entire holder to finishing readiness. Be certain to sand with the grain of wood.

[8] Using either a toothpick or splinter of wood, spread wood glue on the walls of the peg holes. Drive the pegs to the bottom of their drilled holes and allow the glue to dry.

[9] Clean the surface of any excess glue. Sand the ends of the pegs to remove any marks that were made on them when you drove them into the holes.

PROJECT 32: STANDING NECKLACE AND RING HOLDER

The advantage of this design is that it has a place for rings and can be readily moved to any location (Fig. 3-102). It is an ideal size for placement on a chest of drawers or other bedroom furnishings. Also, the design is small enough that a number of holders can be made and placed in different locations.

The project has been designed to hold necklaces of an average length. For longer or shorter ones, cut the support dowel to the appropriate length. Be careful not to make the support piece too long or the holder becomes top heavy and will tip.

Depending upon your own design preferences, you can use either ¼-inch-diameter dowels or small commercial pegs to hold the necklaces. Whichever you select also should be used on the base piece to support rings. The number of dowels or pegs for necklaces is again a matter of need and design. You also can increase the number of ring posts based on need. Figure 3-103 presents the sample project, with dimensions.

Consistent with my bent toward simplicity of design, the lines on this project are rather plain. You might prefer to design a scroll-type top piece, as opposed to a straight one. You also can give the base some balanced scrolls if desired. You can, of course, embellish the top piece with paint or even woodburning. As always, use your imagination and skills to design and embellish the piece to please your tastes.

[1] Use 1-×-4 stock for the entire project. Given the limited amount of wood necessary for the project, you might want to make at least two of them. Measure and cut a piece of 1 × 4 to a length of 13 inches. Next, measure and cut the 5-inch-long base piece from the 13-inch board. The width of the base piece is 3½ inches, which is the standard width of a 1 × 4.

Saw the remaining 8-inch-long piece into two pieces that are 1¾ inches wide and 8 inches long. Select one of these pieces for the top portion of the holder.

[2] Measure and mark the location of the ¼-inch-diameter dowels on the top piece. Refer to Fig. 3-103 for suggested dimensions. Also, measure

Fig. 3-103. Design of the Standing Necklace and Ring Holder.

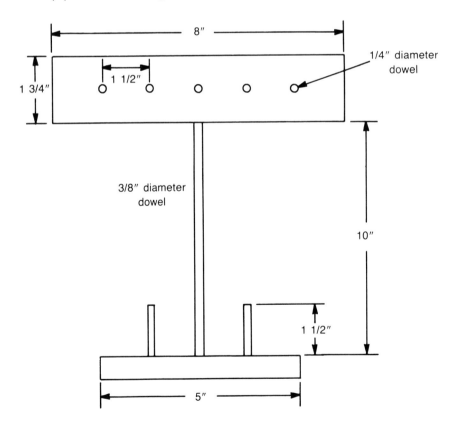

and mark the location of the ring posts on the base piece. Their location should be along the centerline of the piece, about 1 inch from the edges.

[3] Using a ¼-inch-diameter drill bit, drill the holes to a uniform depth. The drilled holes should be at least ¼ inch deep.

[4] Cut five ¼-inch-diameter dowels to a length of at least 1½ inches.

[5] Mark the location of the support dowel on the base piece. It should be in the exact center, in line with the ring posts. Find the center of the top section and mark the location of the support dowel on the bottom edge. The support dowel should be a ⅜-inch-diameter dowel.

[6] Drill the marked locations of the support dowel to a depth of at least ½ inch using a ⅜-inch-diameter wood bit.

[7] Cut the support dowel to a depth of 10 inches.

[8] Rout or sand round the various edges on the top piece and the base.

[9] Using a range of abrasive grits, prepare the surfaces for finishing. Slightly round the ends of all the dowels.

[10] Using either a toothpick or wood splinter, spread glue on the walls of the dowel holes and drive in the dowels. It is not necessary to glue the support dowel. Be certain the dowels are driven all the way into their respective holes. Wipe off any wood glue that is forced from the holes.

PROJECT 33: ADJUSTABLE BOOK ENDS, CAT

This is one of those projects that is fun to make and use. It is especially appropriate for a child's room. Although the project employs a cat design for the book ends (Fig. 3-104), any other animal or configuration can be used. Fruits, or vegetables, or a range of other objects also can be used as the book ends. If you are inclined to painting, carving, or turning, you might want to add the facial details of a cat. I usually drill holes for the eyes. As you plan for the project, consider making the cats a bit more realistic in appearance.

The project holds books that are supported on two dowels and held in place by the two ends. You might want to design the project to a size that will fit on a desktop or a nightstand. I use ¾-inch-diameter dowels for the project, but you can use smaller ones. In part, the dowel size depends on both the length of the holder and the size of the books. You should do some overall design work prior to making the project. Design it in relation to the number of books that will be held in the holder, along with their size and the location of the unit. Figure 3-105 presents the project design and its dimensions.

[1] Use 1-×-6 stock for the cat end pieces.

[2] You need to make a pattern of the cat for the end pieces. Although you can draw one freehand directly onto the board, it is somewhat easier to make one using construction paper. Use the outline in Fig. 3-105 as a guide for your pattern. You might prefer to modify the cat design or even change its dimensions. The pattern should be at least 7 inches high in order to provide adequate support for the books.

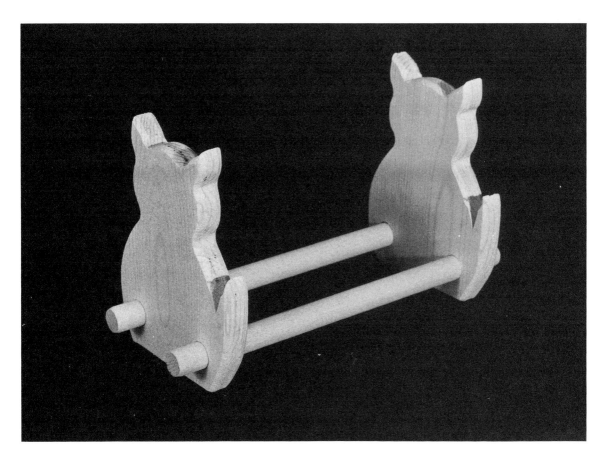

Fig. 3-104. Cat Book Ends.

[3] Measure and cut the end pieces to a length of 8 inches. This length will allow an extra 1 inch for purposes of patterning and cutting. You might need some extra length for the ears of the cat. Trace the end pattern on both boards and cut. A saber saw is effective for cutting the detail in the cat design.

[4] Cut two pieces of ¾-inch-diameter dowel to a length of 12 inches. This length and diameter are the suggested project dimensions. Of course, you might prefer to use other dimensions based on your earlier planning activities.

[5] Carefully layout the location of the two dowels that penetrate the ends. You must drill two ¾-inch-diameter holes through both cats. When the project is assembled, the dowels pass through these holes. Refer to Fig. 3-105 for the approximate location of the dowels. The dowels should be precisely placed so measure and mark the location of the holes before drilling. In part, the placement of the dowels is determined by the size of books that will be placed in the holder.

[6] Use a ¾-inch-diameter wood bit to drill the holes. Be certain to place a support board under the end pieces while you are drilling the holes.

After you have drilled the holes, test the dowels in them for fit. If they are too tight, widen the holes using either abrasive paper or a round wood

152

Side view

Book end

3/4" diameter
dowel

7"

12"

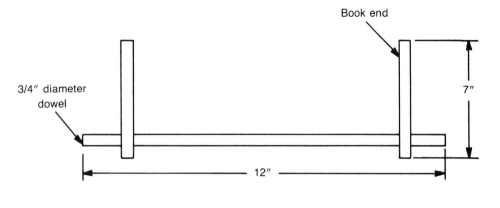

End view

Drilled holes for eyes

7"

5 1/2"

3/4"
dowels

Flat bottom

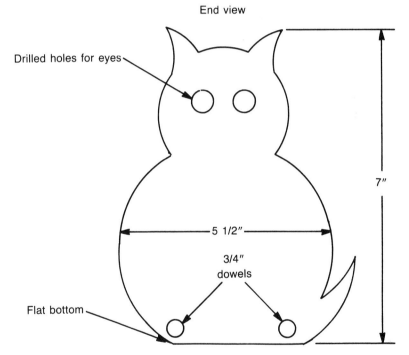

Fig. 3-105. Design of the Cat Book Ends.

rasp. The dowels should move freely in the drilled holes so you can adjust the book ends as needed. Sand the end edges of the dowels round.

[7] Rout or sand the edges on both sides of the cats.

[8] Sand all the edges and surfaces to a finishing readiness.

[9] If desired, drill two holes for eyes in both cats.

Chapter 4

Finishing and Hanging Projects

Finishing pine projects and then hanging or placing them in appropriate locations in the house is also part of the woodworking process. Many, including myself, prefer the actual crafting process. Finishing and hanging the pieces, however, are mandatory tasks and, despite any aversion to these procedures, you must do them.

As you no doubt are aware, the chemical industry has inundated the marketplace with finishing products. Although this variety greatly facilitates the finishing process, it also serves to confuse and often discourage the beginning woodworker. The selection of stains or paints often involves a rather tedious decision-making process. The plethora of oils, lacquers, varnishes, and polyurethanes often serves only to confuse. Although I encourage you to explore this incredible world of chemistry, I also suggest you consider using a few products that I have found helpful. After finishing pine projects for many years, I have identified a number of products and developed a few useful finishing methods.

In addition to the range of advances in finishing products, similar progress has been made in developing very functional devices with which to hang projects. Although a finishing nail driven into the wall is still an effective method, there are numerous alternatives to this hanging procedure. I will present a number of useful devices as well as methods, that will assist you in hanging the range of pine projects that you have crafted.

The major problem in hanging any piece is deciding on its location. Although the crafting process can be filled with great satisfaction, the hanging process can be fraught with grief. Seldom, if ever, have two individuals agreed on the exact location of any item in a household. Compounding the process further are ancillary issues, such as whether the piece is too high or too low, straight or crooked. Although I can assist you in learning about the devices and methods for hanging projects, you are on your own in resolving relational problems that develop. My best recommendation is to learn how to hang pieces and then hang them when no one else is around. This approach has worked well in my household.

REASONS FOR FINISHING

There are two basic reasons for putting some type of finish on the projects that you have crafted. First, wood needs to be protected. This protection is especially important for projects that are placed in the bathroom or other areas where they will be exposed to excessive moisture. Although you cannot make wood waterproof with household-type finishes, you can give it sufficient protection to minimize damage.

This protective function of finishing also serves to protect the wood from other products that would stain or mark it. Chemicals in soaps, alcohol, and a variety of other liquids can stain the wood unless there is some type of finish on its surface. Finishes, especially surface-type finishes, also make cleaning or dusting wood pieces considerably easier. One of the disadvantages of oil-type finishes is that, if not applied properly, they tend to collect dust and are difficult to keep clean.

The second reason for finishing wood projects is decorative. Fortunately, most modern finishing products are manufactured to serve both a protective and decorative function. It is the decorative function, however, that confronts the would-be finisher with the most problems. The selection of colors, whether paint or stain, can be most frustrating. Although they often look appropriate on a manufacturer's color chart, their appearance seems to change radically when they are applied to wood.

An effective procedure in selecting colors is to simply purchase the smallest possible quantity available and test it on a scrap of wood. Although this procedure is usually effective, it often results in a collection of small cans of unwanted stains and paints. When you are doing this type of testing, it is important to remember that pine soaks up both stain and paint very easily. Unlike hardwoods, pine is not always the easiest wood to finish. Its porosity can greatly distort colors, especially with stains.

Tole painters also must decide on finishing products that are compatible with the paints to be used. It is imperative that, if you plan to tole-paint your projects, you check with a tole painter about finishing products. You also might want to review some of the books listed in the Bibliography.

PRELIMINARIES TO FINISHING

Before you apply any finishing products, you must properly prepare the wood's surface. For most pine projects, you must adequately sand the wood and remove all dust. The quality of the final finish is primarily determined by how well the surface has been sanded.

Prior to final sanding of the surfaces, you might want to fill nail holes, cracks, or other areas with a wood filler. There are numerous wood filler products on the market that are usable with pine. You will want to use white or natural color fillers.

Be certain to read the product label on the wood filler you select. The nature of wood fillers requires that you overfill holes or cracks. As the product dries, it tends to shrink. You must sand areas that you have filled after the product is totally dry. Sand the area flush to the wood's surface. Be careful that you sand with the wood grain.

Although areas holding wood filler can be stained, their final appearance is inevitably different from the actual wood. You can distinguish areas that have been packed with filler. In most instances, the difference in appearance is not all that critical. I would advise, however, that you minimize the use of fillers, especially on exposed and highly visible surfaces.

If you prefer an excellent homemade filler, use pine sawdust and white glue. Squeeze a portion of white glue onto a scrap board and stir sawdust into the glue. Stir the mixture until it is a paste, saturated with the sawdust. Force the paste into nail holes or cracks and allow to dry. As with other fillers, it is best to overfill the areas because there is a certain amount of shrinkage when the glue dries.

This type of homemade filler tends to be less conspicuous than some of the commercial fillers. If you use sufficient sawdust, it will stain almost the same as the actual board. Be certain to sand the filler flush to the board's surface.

Another important preliminary, especially if you plan to stain the project, is to remove any excess wood glue from the surfaces. Stain or oil finishes will not penetrate through any dried glue on the wood. Also, closely examine joints and other areas where you used wood glue. If you find dried glue, remove it using 100-grit abrasive paper. Sand with the grain. In some instances, you might need to use a knife to chip away excess glue.

You also must remove sanding dust from all areas of the project before you apply any finishing product. As mentioned earlier, the ideal tool for this procedure is an air compressor and air gun. An effective alternative is to wipe all surfaces with a clean, dry rag. Remove as much dust and other debris as possible. Dampen a portion of another rag with turpentine, and go over all surfaces to remove any remaining dust. Another effective tool for removing dust from a project is a shop vacuum.

An important preliminary activity to finishing is to decide on where to actually do the finishing. The ideal area to do finishing is outside, preferably in a grassy area. The backyard usually has a minimum of dust and maximum of needed ventilation.

If you must do finishing in the garage or basement, be certain that the area is adequately ventilated. Many finishing products are damaging when inhaled. Most are flammable. Some product vapors can actually be explosive.

Do not do any finishing where there is a pilot light or some other type of flame present. Read the label cautions carefully and abide by them. Finishing can be a highly dangerous process. By all means, wear the appropriate breathing device when noted.

TYPES OF FINISHES

Stains. Pine or country projects are generally stained with one of the many colors currently available. As suggested earlier, selecting the appropriate color can be a major task. Stains are usually available with either an oil or water base. My preference is to use an oil-based stain.

If you prefer a light, honey-colored or scrubbed-pine look, one of the maple-colored stains is a good choice. As with all stains, there is considerable variability of colors between manufacturers. You will need to experiment with the various products to find one that you prefer.

I stain most of my pine projects dark. The darker stains tend to blend in with most room decors. I use a Danish walnut color and darken it with a lamp-black universal colorant. You might prefer the stain as it comes from the can. Most paint or hardware stores stock a variety of universal colorants that are compatible with oil-based stains. You might want to try them.

After stirring the stain, add a few small squirts of colorant. Mix the colorant into the stain and then test it on a piece of scrap. If it is still not the desired shade, add more colorant. You can, of course, be a bit more scientific and use a measuring device. You also might want to record the amount of colorant you added for future reference.

Surface Finishes. Although projects can be used with only stain applied to them, the wood is not well protected or very attractive. In most instances, you will want to apply either a surface finish or an oil finish. It is worth noting that many of my pine projects are not stained. Numerous project pictures present items that were finished with either lacquer or oil only. My own preference is not to use stain on pine and, instead, finish it with a clear lacquer and paste wax. Pine is beautiful with only a lacquer finish. The issue is whether or not it will blend with a particular room decor.

As with stains and paints, there is an endless array of surface finishing products on the market. Without some prior knowledge, it is almost overwhelming to be confronted with the diversity of products. In addition to the many varnishes available, there are numerous polyurethanes that can be effectively used on pine.

As indicated, my preference is to use a clean lacquer finish on pine projects. I have used Deft, a clear lacquer, for many years on both pine and hardwood projects. Unlike most varnishes and polyurethanes, lacquers dry very quickly. They are ideal for finishing when you do not have a dust-free environment. Lacquers can be used on stained or unfinished pine with equally good results. If a water-resistant finish is desired, simply increase the number of coats applied. As with all finishing products, read the directions.

Oil Finishes. For an oil finish, I use Watco Danish Oil Finish. Unlike surface finishes, oil finishes are absorbed into the wood. There are numerous other excellent oil finishes on the market that can be used on either stained or unfinished pine. For an inexpensive oil finish, use boiled linseed oil. An oil finish on a pine project, whether stained or not, is extremely attractive.

There are numerous oil finishes that can be used on cutting boards, bowls, or other projects that are to be used with food. Any finishing product that is used should be nontoxic. Watco Danish Oil Finish can be used because it is nontoxic when dry. I use mineral oil on cutting boards and spoons. A good procedure is to warm the wood and rub the oil into it. Use several treatments. Vegetable oil is not recommended. In some instances, your own experience might be the preferable way to finish projects that will be used with food.

Paints. The use of paints, either oil based or latex, is another way to finish your projects. Although my preference is to use latex, you might prefer the oil paints. As with stain, the range of colors can be very confusing. You might prefer to use colors already present in your house. There is also a selection of Early American colors available from several mail-order suppliers. Pine accepts paint very well, and you might want to consider its use on a number of your projects.

FINISHING PROCEDURES

Although you will develop your own procedures to finish pine projects, it seems appropriate to detail how I do it. I am confident there are better and more effective methods; however, the following procedures have worked well for me when finishing pine projects.

Whenever I am finishing, I spread several layers of newspaper on the surface where I will be working. In that I am somewhat careless when applying stain, the paper is critical. In addition to newspaper, I have several scraps of pine available on which the freshly stained project can be placed to dry. If you leave the stained piece on the newspapers, the newsprint will come off and be absorbed by the wood.

Be certain your finishing area is well ventilated if you are not doing the finishing outside. You might want to use one of the various masks that filter the toxic fumes. If you are using an oil-based stain, you also might want to wear rubber or plastic gloves. I generally use surgical gloves, which are thicker and stronger than the ones available in paint stores. Gloves prevent the stain from getting all over your hands. They also eliminate the need to use turpentine or other stain removers on your skin.

For applying the stain, I use either a 1- or 2-inch-wide brush. As a rule, I purchase inexpensive brushes and then throw them away when the project is done. I have found that with stain, the type and quality of the brush is not all that critical. You also can use a rag for applying the stain. Use a rag that is not loaded with lint. You do not want fabric remains all over your project.

When you are applying the stain with a brush, simply spread it around on the project's various surfaces. I tend to use a lot of stain and really slop it on the wood. The amount of stain used does not affect the color of the project. More does not make it darker. Be certain all the surfaces are adequately covered. You do not need to worry about brush marks with stain.

I usually stain the back portion of the project first. If it is a cabinet, I do the inside first. It is best to simply pick up the project and spread the stain. I make the process as simple as possible. Wear an apron or old clothes so you can hold the piece in your lap while you are spreading the stain.

Areas on the project that have end grains I stain last. End grain on the wood tends to absorb stain like a sponge. As a result, they often are somewhat darker in appearance. To adequately cover the end-grain areas, you often need to force stain in with the brush. There is little you can do to prevent the end grain from absorbing the stain. It is the nature of pine to be porous.

When the entire project is covered with stain, I place it on the wood scraps for a few minutes. Usually the label directions will indicate how long you should allow the stain to dry. I begin wiping the stain off while it is still wet. If you allow the stain to dry totally, the surface will be blotchy looking. You can always restain the project if necessary.

Use lint-free rags to wipe off the stain. I tend to rub the surface lightly as I wipe off the stain. Wipe with the wood grain. Do not press or rub too hard, or you will remove all the stain. Fold a portion of the rag to get into the various corners of the project. You want all the excess stain removed. When wiping is complete, place the project on scraps and allow it to dry thoroughly. Drying time varies depending upon the product, temperature, and humidity. Generally, the label directions will indicate a time frame for proper drying.

Because rags and newspaper used in finishing can combust spontaneously, you should dispose of them immediately. If you cannot burn them, spread them outside until you can dispose of them properly. By all means, do not roll them into a ball and toss them in a corner. These procedures also apply to the clothes you were wearing if they are covered with stain.

When the stain is dry, I apply a surface finish to the project. As indicated, I prefer using Deft, a high-quality lacquer. When preparing to apply the lacquer, I again spread newspaper and use scraps of wood. You will want to wear an appropriate breathing device when you are using lacquer.

Since lacquers dry very quickly, they are ideal for the hobbyist finisher. They can be used in the kinds of areas most people do their finishing. My shop is in the garage and it is a perpetual mess. It is by no means a dust-free environment. I have found that Deft usually dries before it can begin attracting too much dust. As always, read the directions on the product before you use it.

Although there are many high-quality brushes available for use with lacquers, I generally purchase the most inexpensive. Lacquer spreads easily and brush marks are generally not a problem. You will find that the cheaper brushes tend to lose a few bristles during use. I simply pick them off the surface and brush over the area. Rather than clean the brush when finished, I simply discard it. You can use lacquer thinner to clean brushes if you prefer. It also will clean lacquer from your hands. This product is also dangerous and should be used according to label directions.

Few projects lend themselves to being lacquered entirely in one step.

Normally you will need to finish a portion of the project at a time. As a rule, I finish the exposed areas first. For example, on a mirror, I finish the front surface and the edges first. When these are done, I finish the back surface. This type of procedure varies from project to project.

As with stain, the end grains tend to absorb the lacquer very quickly. You will need to spread additional coats on the various end-grain areas of the project. It is almost impossible to totally fill the end grains with lacquer.

As a rule, I put three to four coats of Deft on most projects. For pieces that will be used in the bathroom or around moisture, I put on additional coats. You would be well advised to consult the label directions for projects that will be exposed to water and other liquids.

When the lacquer is dry, I go over all surfaces with (0000) steel wool. The steel wool removes any dust particles that have stuck to the surface. It also cuts the gloss of the lacquer and makes its appearance somewhat dull. Steel wool greatly enhances the final finish. Depending upon the project, I sometimes use steel wool between coats of lacquer. Do not rub too hard or you will cut through the finish with the wool. Do not use steel wool on end grain because the grain tends to pull out hairs that attach themselves to the wood. Using a rag or air gun, remove all the strands of steel wool left on the project's surface.

As a final procedure, I rub all surfaces, except the end grain, with paste wax. There are numerous excellent paste waxes on the market. I use clear Trewax paste wax, clear Butcher's Wax paste wax, or Johnson's paste wax. Read the label directions on the can and use accordingly. These are excellent waxes to use on your projects on an ongoing basis. They are especially useful for projects used in the bathroom or where moisture is present. Incidentally, flannel rags are very effective for polishing the waxed surfaces.

After you have finished a mirror frame, glue the mirror into the frame using white glue. Do not spread wax in the recessed mirror area or the glue will not hold. Apply the glue between the edge of the mirror and the recessed area of the frame. Then cover the back of the mirror and the recessed area with a piece of construction paper. Measure and cut the paper to the needed dimensions. Spread white glue on the edge of the paper and press in place. For procedures on cutting mirror glass, refer to Project 11.

HANGING DEVICES AND PROCEDURES

With few exceptions, the process of hanging your wood projects is not a matter of concern until you are completely done with the finishing process. You prepared some pieces for hanging during the crafting process. For example, you drilled hanging holes through the support pieces of shelves. You might or might not want to use these holes to hang your items after exploring some other options for hanging projects.

The major consideration in hanging your projects is the kind of walls you have in your house or apartment. Another variable that affects hanging is whether or not you want to be able to remove your wood pieces if and when you move. Related to this issue if you are an apartment dweller, are any restrictions you have on how you can hang things on the walls. I will deal with some of these concerns in hanging projects and also a few tips on patching holes.

Most new housing construction has what is generally called *drywall construction*. Simply stated, this usually means that your walls are a kind of plaster board that does not lend itself to simply hanging something with a nail. This is the kind of wall that tends to crumble when you try to hang something on it. Drywall usually has a paper kind of surface and is anywhere from ½ to ¾ inch thick. This type of wall material makes for great housing, but is lousy stuff for trying to hang things.

The other kind of walls, frequently found in older homes, are plaster walls. These walls are usually very hard and thick, and when you drive a nail into them, the plaster tends to fall away around the nail. The wall tends to powder and chip when you try to drive a nail into it. Plaster walls can be miserable things on which to hang anything. Incidentally, if you do want to drive a nail into a plaster wall, place a piece of transparent tape over the spot where the nail is to be driven. The tape tends to hold the plaster material in place and thus support the nail.

One piece of information that might or might not prove helpful in hanging things is to remember that behind the walls are usually 2-×-4 studs. Most new construction has a stud every 16 inches, while older homes are often built with 20 inches or more between the studs. If you are lucky enough to have studs in the approximate area where you want to hang something, you might want to use them. They can be especially useful when you are hanging a shelf that will carry a considerable amount of weight.

Frequently you can locate the studs, on drywall construction at least, by looking for small indentations in the wall's surface. They generally run from the floor to the ceiling. These little pot marks are where the plaster board was nailed to the stud, each one representing a nail head that was not patched over very well.

You also can buy a stud finder to use in locating the studs in the walls. Essentially, a stud finder is a small magnet that elevates a red pointer when contact is made over the head of a nail. I have not been overly successful in finding studs with these devices.

Normally, when I need to locate a stud for hanging something, I find myself looking for nail holes and tapping the wall with a knuckle. The sound when a stud is present is distinctly different from the hollow sound between studs. To confirm the stud, using a small finishing nail, I punch a hole through the wall. Usually these procedures will result in locating a stud for hanging items. You then can measure from this stud to locate other studs that you might need.

You can fill holes in the wall easily with either spackling paste or patching compound. This material is like putty and usually is white in color. If you have painted walls, you can mix a little paint into some of the spackling paste

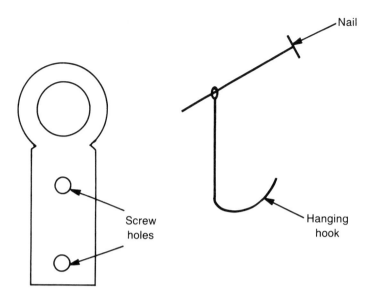

before you fill the hole. This kind of material is excellent for patching nail holes that remain when you remove items from the wall. As always, read the directions on the can prior to using.

I have found that the easiest way to hang wood items when screws or nails cannot be driven into studs is to use brass hangers and picture hooks (Fig. 4-1). Both of these items are generally available at local hardware stores or from mail-order suppliers. Screw the brass hangers on the back of the project with the round top extending above the surface. Figure 4-2 depicts how the hangers appear when placed on the back of a shelf. The picture hooks slide through the hanger holes and hold the unit to the wall.

Fig. 4-1. Brass hangers and picture hooks.

Fig. 4-2. Brass hangers on shelf.

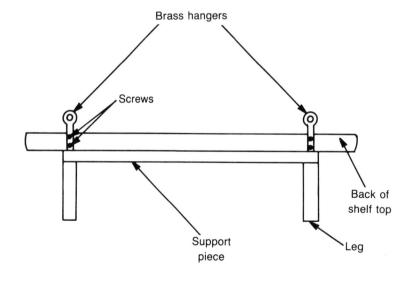

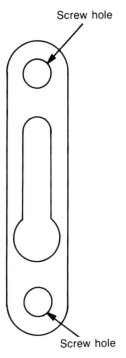

Screw hole

Screw hole

Fig. 4-3. Keyhole mounting plate.

Fig. 4-4. Keyhole plate on shelf legs.

To hang a shelf using these devices, place the unit against the wall at the exact location desired. Use a small torpedo level, placed on the shelf top's surface, to level the unit. Move one end of the shelf up and down until the bubble in the level vial is between the two lines, indicating that the shelf is level. Using a pencil, mark the wall at the top edge of both brass hangers. These two points are where you need to drive the picture hooks into the wall. As the devices indicate, the picture-hook nails need to be driven into the wall at an angle.

Another type of hanging device that is especially effective for shelves is a keyhole mounting plate (Fig. 4-3). Unlike the brass hangers and picture hooks, when these devices are routed and secured in place on the back surfaces of shelf legs, they cannot be seen. The keyholes in the plates are designed to slide over the head of a screw or nail that penetrates a wall or wood surface, thus preventing the shelf from sliding off the nails or screws.

An effective device to use with the keyhole-mounting plate, especially on drywall construction, is a Molly bolt or Molly jack nut. Locate a pack of them in a hardware store and read the directions on the package. The Molly bolt comes in various lengths. Once secured to the wall, only the actual holding bolt can be removed. Part of the device remains permanently secured in the wall. The Molly bolt is an excellent device for hanging projects, but does require a bit more time, tools, and accuracy. Look over a package of them before making a decision regarding their use. Incidentally, the Molly bolt is also an excellent device if you want to hang a project on an inside, hollow-core door.

For placement of the keyhole plates on the legs of a shelf, you need to rout a ⅝-inch-wide trench that is approximately 1⅝ inches long. The length of the trench is determined by the actual length of the plate. Rout the trench to a depth of at least 3⁄16 inch. If you have used a support piece in the shelf design, the routed area should be below it. If you have not used a support piece, rout the trenches near the top edge of the legs (Fig. 4-4). You also can rout the trench beginning in the back edge of the shelf top and extending down into the leg.

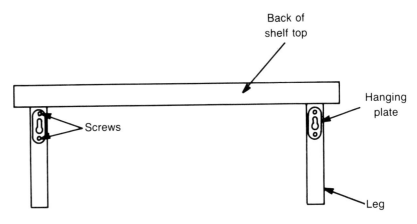

Back of
shelf top

Hanging
plate

Screws

Leg

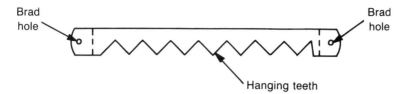

Brad hole

Brad hole

Hanging teeth

Fig. 4-5. Saw tooth hanger.

The trench is best routed using a ⅝-inch-diameter straight router bit on a table-mounted router. A properly aligned fence is mandatory for routing the two trenches. After the routing is complete, drill two ⅜-inch holes in each trench. The holes should overlap each other. The drilled holes allow the head of the screw or nail to penetrate through the plate and into the leg. Using ½-×-5-inch flat-head wood screws, secure the plates into the trenches.

Another hanging device that is effective with mirrors or other small projects is the saw tooth hanger (Fig. 4-5). Center the sawtooth at the top back of a project and secure it in place with two small brads. Then place the sawtooth on a nail or screw in the wall or other surface. You can make the project hang straight by placing the proper tooth area over the nail. These devices are available in a range of lengths and are inexpensive. You can obtain them from most hardware stores or mail-order suppliers.

For small mirrors and sometimes even T Shelves, you can use a small, brass picture hanger and escutcheon pins (Fig. 4-6). Escutcheon pins are simply small brass brads with a round head. They are available in a range of lengths and diameters. These smaller hangers should be used only on projects that are not too heavy. They are excellent for hanging small Scrap Mirrors or similar projects.

On occasion, you might want to use decorative ring hangers on mirrors or other small projects. Center the hanger on the top edge of a frame and screw it in place (Fig. 4-7). After the ring is in place on the project, hang it on a nail extending from the wall or other surface. The nail needs to extend far enough from the wall so that the ring can fit over its head. There is a large variety of this type of hanger on the market, and usually they are available in various sizes at local hardware or discount stores.

Another device with which I have had some success is a keyhole router bit (Fig. 4-8). The bit allows you to rout a keyhole in the back surface of a project. As with the keyhole plate hanger, you simply slip the slot over a nail or screw head and it is secured in place. When the bit is set for a ⅜-inch depth of cut, it makes the slot as it moves forward in the wood. You will want to hold the router and make the rout freehand with this bit. The procedure takes some practice, but the keyhole router bit is an effective device for preparing projects for hanging.

Although not a device as such, double-faced tape also can be used to hang projects. Usually the tape is available in either rolls or small squares. As its name implies, it is sticky on both surfaces. Place a small strip or square of tape onto the back surface of the project. Remove the protective covering from the other surface and set the project in place. The tape bond is very

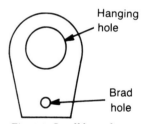

Hanging hole

Brad hole

Fig. 4-6. Small brass hanger.

Fig. 4-7. Decorative ring hanger.

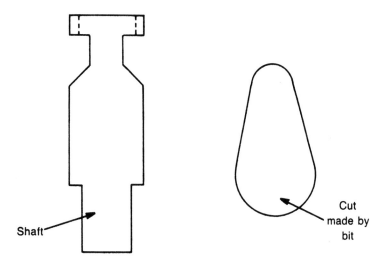

Shaft

Cut
made by
bit

Fig. 4-8. Keyhole router bit.   strong when in place, especially on smooth surfaces. You will find, however, that the tape can remove paint when you pull it off a surface.

As you are confronted with the task of hanging your small pine projects, you will find that there are other devices and techniques for hanging them. I try to browse in hardware stores or review catalogs looking for new and more effective ways to hang projects. It is an excellent way to learn more about what is available to do a job that no one particularly enjoys.

Appendices

Appendix:
Suppliers and Magazines

MAIL-ORDER SUPPLIERS

The following list of mail-order suppliers is but a sampling of companies that specialize in crafting supplies, woodworking tools, and related accessories. Each company has a mail-order catalog and, in some instances, a toll-free telephone number to facilitate your ordering. While some companies provide free mail-order catalogs, others have a moderate change. It is best to write the company and request information on its catalog.

Constantine
2050 Eastchester Road
Bronx, NY 10461

Craftsman
1735 W. Cortland Ct.
Addison, IL 60101

The Fine Tool Shops, Inc.
20 Backus Ave.
P.O. Box 1262
Danbury, CT 06810

Frog Tool Co., Ltd.
P.O. Box 8325
Chicago, IL 60680

Klockit
P.O. Box 629
Lake Geneva, WI 53147

Meisel Hardware Specialties
P.O. Box 258
Mound, MN 55364

Sears, Roebuck and Co.
Sears Tower
Chicago, IL 60684

Seven Corners Ace Hardware, Inc.
216 West 7th St.
St. Paul, MN 55102

Highland Hardware
1045 N. Highland Ave., NE
Atlanta, GA 30306

Hiller Hardware Co.
P.O. Box 1762
Columbia, SC 29202

Woodcraft
41 Atlantic Ave.
P.O. Box 4000
Woburn, MA 01888

The Woodworkers' Store
21801 Industrial Blvd.
Rogers, MN 55374

Trend-Lines
375 Beacham St.
P.O. Box 6447
Chelsea, MA 02150

Warren Tool Co., Inc.
Rt. 1, P.O. Box 14
Rhinebeck, NY 12572

Woodworkers Supply of New
Mexico
5604 Alameda, NE
Albuquerque, NM 87113

Woodworks
4013-A Clay Ave.
Ft. Worth, TX 76117

WOODWORKING MAGAZINES

The following list of magazines is for those interested in all facets of woodworking. For subscription information, write to the addresses given.

The American Woodworker
P.O. Box 1408
Hendersonville, TN 37077

Fine Woodworking
The Taunton Press, Inc.
P.O. Box 355
Newton, CT 06470

The Mallet
National Carvers Museum
Foundation
14960 Woodcarver Rd.
Monument, CO 80132

Wood
Better Homes and Gardens
P.O. Box 10693
Des Moines, IA 50380

Bibliography

Berry, James B. *Wood Identification*. New York: Dover Publications, Inc., 1966.

Clifford, Jerrold R. *Basic Woodworking and Carpentry*. Blue Ridge Summit, PA.: TAB BOOKS, Inc., 1980.

Constantine, Albert Jr. *Know Your Woods*. New York: Charles Scribner's Sons, 1959.

Daniele, Joseph. *Building Early American Furniture*. Harrisburg, PA.: Stackpole Books, 1974.

Edlin, Herbert L. *What Wood Is That?* New York: The Viking Press, 1969.

Fraser, B. Kay. *Tole Painting*. New York: Sterling, 1971.

Groneman, Chris H. *General Woodworking*. New York: McGraw-Hill Book Co., 1971.

Harrar, E.S. *Hough's Encyclopedia of American Woods*. 13 volumes. New York: Robert Speller and Sons, 1957.

Hauser, Priscilla. *Tole and Decorative Painting*. New York: Van Nostrand Reinhold Co., 1977.

Howard, Joyce. *New Tole and Folk Art Designs*. Radnor, PA.: Chilton Book Co., 1979.

Kellell, Russell H. *The Pine Furniture of Early New England*. New York: Dover Publications, Inc., 1956.

Midkiff, Pat. *The Complete Book of Stenciling*. New York: Sterling, 1978.

Pain, F. *The Practical Wood Turner*. New York: Drake Publishers, Inc., 1974.

Schiffer, Nancy and Herbert. *Woods We Live With*. Exton, Pa.: Schiffer Publishing, Ltd., 1977.

Sloane, Eric. *Reverence for Wood*. New York: Ballantine Books, 1965.

Tangerman, E.J. *Whittling and Woodcarving*. New York: Dover Publications, Inc., 1936.

Index

Index

Edited by Suzanne L. Cheatle

Other Bestsellers From TAB

☐ **THE PORTABLE ROUTER BOOK—**
R. J. DeCristoforo

If you've always thought of your portable router as a pretty unexciting tool, capable of little more than producing decorative edges on certain types of woodworking projects . . . then this book is just what you need to start taking advantage of all the creative possibilities that the router can really offer! Plus, you'll find how-to's for making your own router stands, jigs, fixtures and guides for use in creating such special effects as fluting, reeding, tapering, and peripheral cutting. 368 pp., 466 illus.

Paper $14.95   **Hard $24.95**
Book No. 2869

☐ **SMALL ENGINES: OPERATION, MAINTENANCE**
AND REPAIR—AAVIM

This time-, money-, and aggravation-saving sourcebook shows how you can service, operate, maintain, and repair any air-cooled, spark-ignition, one-half to approximately 15 horsepower engine yourself . . . and save hundreds of dollars in repair bills! If you wish to expand your knowledge beyond the service and operation of small engines, part two briefs you on the procedures and techniques you need to know to tackle major maintenance and repair work. 288 pp., 529 illus., 8 1/2″ × 11″.

Paper $14.95   **Hard $24.95**
Book No. 2813

☐ **133 *USEFUL* PROJECTS FOR THE**
WOODWORKER—*School Shop Magazine*

A wealth of information for beginning and advanced hobbyists . . . tools, techniques, and dozens of exciting projects. Here's a handbook that deserves a permanent spot on every woodworker's tool bench. Packed with show-how illustrations and material lists, this invaluable guide provides you with a wide variety of useful, and fun-to-make woodworking projects: a spice rack, a wall clock, a plant stand, a cutting board, a wooden chest, a magazine rack, a serving cart, a child's playhouse, and more! 160 pp., 289 illus.

Paper $12.95   **Hard $19.95**
Book No. 2783

☐ **MASTER HANDBOOK OF WOODWORKING TECH-**
NIQUES AND PROJECTS—2nd Edition—Percy W.
Blandford

This classic guide to traditional furniture crafting is now completely updated to include the very latest methods, materials, tools, equipment, and techniques . . . while continuing to stress the importance of fine craftsmanship. Actual projects from simple bookcases, chests, and stools to advanced designs like a Queen Anne table and a glass-fronted cupboard are included. 368 pp., 349 illus.

Paper $14.95   **Hard $25.95**
Book No. 2744

☐ **DREAM HOMES: 66 PLANS TO MAKE YOUR**
DREAMS COME TRUE—Jerold L. Axelrod, Architect

If you are planning on—or just dreaming of—building a new home, you will find this book completely fascinating. Compiled by a well-known architect whose home designs have been featured regularly in the syndicated "House of the Week" and *Home* magazine, this beautifully bound volume presents one of the finest collections of luxury home designs ever assembled in a single volume! 88 pp., 201 illus., 8 1/2″ × 11″ Extra Large Format. 20 Full-Color Pages.

Paper $16.95   **Hard $29.95**
Book No. 2829

☐ **HOME PLUMBING MADE EASY: AN ILLUSTRATED**
MANUAL—James L. Kittle

Here, in one heavily illustrated, easy-to-follow volume, is all the how-to-do-it information needed to perform almost any home plumbing job, in both water and waste disposal systems. Whether you want to learn something about household plumbing so you can save time and money next time a problem occurs, or you're thinking of making major plumbing or septic additions or repairs to your home, this is the place to start! 272 pp., 250 illus.

Paper $14.95   **Hard $24.95**
Book No. 2797

☐ **77 ONE-WEEKEND WOODWORKING PROJECTS—**
Percy W. Blandford

Let this guide put the fun back into your hobby! Overflowing with step-by-step instructions, easy-to-follow illustrations, dimensioned drawings, and material lists, this indispensable guide includes plans for 77 projects: tables, racks and shelves, a take-down book rack, corner shelves, a vase stand, beds and cabinets, yard and garden projects, toys, games and puzzles, tools, and more. 304 pp., 226 illus.

Paper $14.95   **Hard $23.95**
Book No. 2774

☐ **THE COMPLETE BOOK OF BATHROOMS—Judy**
and Dan Ramsey and Charles Self

Simple redecorating tricks . . . remodeling advice . . . plumbing techniques . . . it's all here. Find literally hundreds of photographs, drawings, and floorplans to help you decide exactly what kind of remodeling project you'd like to undertake; plus, step-by-step directions for accomplishing your remodeling goals. It's all designed to save you time and money on your bathroom renovations! 368 pp., 474 illus.

Paper $15.95   **Book No. 2708**

Other Bestsellers From TAB

☐ **79 FURNITURE PROJECTS FOR EVERY ROOM—Percy W. Blandford**

Just imagine your entire home filled with beautiful, hand-crafted furniture! Elegant chairs, tables, and sofas, a hand-finished corner cupboard, luxurious beds and chests, and more! With the hands-on instructions and step-by-step project plans included here, you'll be able to build beautiful furniture for any room . . . or every room in your home . . . at a fraction of the store-bought cost! 384 pp., 292 illus.

Paper $16.95   Hard $24.95
Book No. 2704

☐ **BASIC ROOF FRAMING—Benjamin Barnow**

Would a new gambrel roof make your home more attractive . . . and increase its value? Want to enlarge your attic with dormers to add to your family's living space? Or are you thinking of building an addition to your home? Then this is a sourcebook that will save you hundreds, maybe thousands of dollars in contractor's costs by showing how even a novice carpenter can successfully master the art of roof framing! 192 pp., 250 illus.

Paper $11.95   Hard $19.95
Book No. 2677

☐ **66 FAMILY HANDYMAN® WOOD PROJECTS—Editors of Family Handyman®**

Here are 66 practical, imaginative, and decorative projects . . . literally something for every home and every woodworking skill level from novice to advanced cabinetmaker! You'll find complete step-by-step plans for room dividers, a free-standing corner bench, china/book cabinets, coffee tables, desk and storage units, a built-in sewing center, even your own Shaker furniture reproductions! 210 pp., 306 illus.

Paper $14.95   Book No. 2632

☐ **THE FRUGAL WOODWORKER—Rick Liftig**

Who says you need an elaborate workshop to fully enjoy your woodworking hobby? And who says you have to spend a small fortune on expensive materials to produce pro-quality furniture? *Certainly not Rick Liftig!* And neither will you after you get a look at the expert advice, money-saving tips, and practical low-cost projects included in his exciting new woodworking guide: *The Frugal Woodworker!* You'll find invaluable advice on where and how to acquire wood at bargain prices, even for free! 240 pp., 188 illus.

Paper $12.95   Hard $22.95
Book No. 2702

☐ **PLANNING AND BUILDING FENCES AND GATES—AAVIM**

This colorfully illustrated guide gives you all the expert, step-by-step guidelines and instructions you need to plan and build durable, cost-effective fences and gates. You will be able to design and construct just about any kind of fence you can think of—barbed wire, woven wire, cable wire, mesh wire, board fences, electric fences, gates, and much more! 192 pp., 356 illus., 8 1/2″ × 11″, 2-Color Throughout.

Paper $14.95   Book No. 2643

☐ **THE WOODTURNER'S BIBLE—2nd Edition—Percy W. Blandford**

All the hands-on instruction and project plans you need are in this sourcebook that hundreds of hobbyists and professional woodcrafters consider the most complete guide to woodturning tools and techniques available. And now, this extraordinary guide has been completely revised, updated, and greatly expanded to include a wealth of new information, projects, even directions for building your own low-cost wood-turning lathe! 400 pp., 313 illus.

Paper $16.95   Hard $24.95
Book No. 1954

*Prices subject to change without notice.